DANIEL
O'CONNELL
PORTRAIT OF A RADICAL

RTE
— THE THOMAS DAVIS LECTURES —

DANIEL O'CONNELL

PORTRAIT OF A RADICAL

Edited by Kevin B. Nowlan
and Maurice R. O'Connell

Appletree Press

First published and printed in 1984 by
The Appletree Press Ltd
7 James Street South
Belfast BT2 8DL

British Library Cataloguing in Publication Data
Daniel O'Connell
  1. O'Connell, Daniel   2. Politicians—
Ireland—Biography   3. Lawyers—Ireland
—Biography
I. Nowlan, Kevin B.   II. O'Connell,
Maurice R.
941.5081'092'4   DA950.22

ISBN 0-86281-122-8

RTE
— THE THOMAS DAVIS LECTURES —

DANIEL O'CONNELL

PORTRAIT OF A RADICAL

Edited by Kevin B. Nowlan
and Maurice R. O'Connell

Appletree Press

First published and printed in 1984 by
The Appletree Press Ltd
7 James Street South
Belfast BT2 8DL

British Library Cataloguing in Publication Data
Daniel O'Connell
  1. O'Connell, Daniel   2. Politicians—
  Ireland—Biography   3. Lawyers—Ireland
  —Biography
  I. Nowlan, Kevin B.   II. O'Connell,
  Maurice R.
  941.5081'092'4   DA950.22

ISBN 0-86281-122-8

Contents

Introduction

In the spring of 1975, Radio Telefis Eireann marked the bicentenary of the birth of Daniel O'Connell by broadcasting a series of Thomas Davis Lectures assessing his historical significance. These lectures, in a revised form, are published in this present volume.

We are indebted to Mr Michael Littleton, the general editor of the Thomas Davis Lectures, for his advice and co-operation. We would like to record our appreciation of the generosity of Allied Irish Banks Limited for a subvention in aid of publication and we wish to express our gratitude to the late Declan Dwyer, of Cork, for taking a practical interest in securing the publication of these lectures.

We believe that these studies will help to put in a clearer perspective the place of Daniel O'Connell in the shaping of modern Irish nationalism and in the movement for liberal democracy in the nineteenth century world.

Kevin B. Nowlan
Maurice R. O'Connell

1

O'Connell and Irish Nationalism

Kevin B. Nowlan

Daniel O'Connell probably more than any other major figure in modern Irish history has been the victim of the shifts in popular attitudes to nationalism and its significance. Regarded at one time as the Liberator, the unquestioned leader of his people, he was destined to become the object of criticism from a more advanced school of nationalists. To achieve something like a balanced view of O'Connell, it is essential to turn from these later opinions and look at him in the context of his own time, within the political and social limitations of his age.

The Union of 1801 between Great Britain and Ireland came about as a means of consolidating the political and economic links between the two countries, at a time when Napoleonic France was a constant threat to British interests and when it seemed, too, that French revolutionary ideas would secure a lasting influence on Ireland. It was argued, as well, that the Union would not only help to defeat the revolutionary elements in Ireland, but open the way for Catholic Emancipation, since the Irish Catholics could never achieve a majority position within the new United Kingdom and so could not endanger the Protestant character of the British constitution. The advocates of the Union spoke of a new prosperity for Ireland, but the high hopes for the Union were not to be realised on the scale they had envisaged. Though the nineteenth century was to see an impressive expansion in economic activity in the north-eastern counties, the Union did not bring with it those social and political changes which might have saved Irish society from the chaos and suffering of the Great Famine. Many of the basic defects in Irish society had a long history predating the Union, but it was in a post-union context that Ireland was to experience great and prolonged social distress.

Again, among the Catholic Irish, in the wake of the troubles of the seventeen-nineties, there were those who hoped that Westminster would be more prompt in meeting their grievances than the old ascendancy Parliament in Ireland. Their expectations met with no early reward. The dissatisfaction among the Irish Catholics was a basic factor in understanding the rise of Daniel O'Connell.

O'Connell came out of an eighteenth century world. His family, though Catholic, had survived as landlords and, like so many other such families in the more remote parts of the country, had links with the continent, especially with pre-revolutionary monarchist France. O'Connell's world was to a considerable extent still a Gaelic world and it is evident from his whole career that he had a shrewd insight into the minds and ways of the people. But he was also a lawyer in the English Common Law tradition and again, we know that his political principles and methods owed a great deal to British parliamentary conventions. The French Revolution was quite alien to his ways, and even before his call to the Bar, his deep conservatism on some issues was well illustrated by his reaction to the presence of a French fleet in Bantry Bay, in December 1796. His comments to his Uncle Maurice, the famous "Hunting Cap", was that the threatened invasion, if successful, "should have shook the foundations of all property, would have destroyed our profession (Law) root and branch".[1]

His dislike of the anti-clerical, levelling French revolutionaries was, perhaps, an expression of his respect for the traditions of Grattan and Henry Flood, for the idea of a Kingdom of Ireland with its own Parliament suitably reformed and thrown open to Catholics. The link with the Crown was an essential part of such thinking, and O'Connell was by no means alone in this.

For Daniel O'Connell the two great objectives, in political terms, were the repeal of the Act of Union and the winning of a satisfactory status for the Irish Catholics. Even before the passing of the Act of Union, the young lawyer had denounced the "extinction of the liberty, the constitution and even the name of Ireland." But the question of repeal in the opening years of the nineteenth century had not the same emotional appeal in Ireland as the demand for Catholic Emancipation. The Union was still new and untried. O'Connell realised the practical limitations inherent in the situation and he shaped his formidable and astute plans accordingly. His thinking on these matters emerges well in a speech which he made as early as June 1813:

I desire the restoration of our Irish parliament; I would sacrifice my existence to restore to Ireland her independent legislature; but I do *not* desire to restore precisely such a parliament as she had before. No: the act of restoration necessarily implies a reformation ... [our enemies] delay the liberties of the Catholic, but they compensate us most amply, because they advance the restoration of Ireland; by leaving one cause of agitation [Emancipation] they have created ... a public mind and a public spirit.[2]

O'Connell rapidly made his name as an outstanding lawyer in the opening years of the nineteenth century and with almost equal rapidity he became a leading and ultimately the dominating figure among the advocates of Catholic rights. Between 1808, when he assumed a significant role in the old Catholic committee, and the early eighteen-twenties, he helped to bring a new life and a popular dimension to the agitation. A more controversial note was struck, the many grievances of the people were emphasised, and he made it clear that he was an advocate not merely of Catholic rights but of parliamentary reform as well.

The foundation of the Catholic Association, in 1823, which rapidly won the support of the Catholic clergy, and O'Connell's promotion of the "Catholic Rent" in 1824, secured not merely a substantial fighting fund for the Association but also made possible a mass membership. The cost was low: a subscription of one penny per month. The issue of Catholic Emancipation came quickly to mean more than simply the admission of a few wealthy Catholics to Parliament. It came to symbolise all the aspirations of the Irish Catholics in social and political terms. The careful, effective organisation of the population, and the steady aid of the priests defeated the efforts of the Government, now thoroughly alarmed, to destroy the Association. Its official suppression, in 1825, proved to be a futile gesture as ways were quickly found to establish a new Catholic Association which complied with the letter of the law. The Association was a formidable weapon and O'Connell was to use mass popular support in a new and remarkable way, but his strategy did not involve physical force. The revolt of the Irish rural voters from 1826 onwards, by refusing to obey their landlords' directions in certain key elections, was a measure of the new power which had emerged in Irish political life.

In itself, Catholic Emancipation, finally granted in 1829, brought with it few significant short-term changes. Already before 1829, most of the legal restraints on the Catholics had been repealed and now those Catholics, who could afford it and could win a seat in Parliament, were permitted to enjoy the privilege. A political lesson, however, had been taught. Mass opinion could be brought to bear effectively even on a Tory administration. Against this must be set the reality of the Irish situation in social terms. For many decades after 1829, the Irish Catholic would remain in an inferior position in relation to public employment and the control of wealth. The eighteen-thirties and forties were to see some improvements, but the rate of progress remained slow and hesitant.

When all of these factors are taken into account along with the many evils of the Irish land system and the problem of widespread poverty, it is not surprising that the pattern of political development in Ireland differed so considerably from that in the rest of the United Kingdom. While issues such as Free Trade and Chartism dominated the political scene in Britain, in Ireland neither issue made any real impact. In the early eighteen-thirties and even more so from 1840 onwards, the demand for the repeal of the Act of Union and the restoration of the Irish Parliament determined the character of Irish politics. In the shaping of modern Irish nationalism, it was to be a major part of O'Connell's contribution that he and his supporters kept Repeal as a central theme in Irish affairs at this important and decisive period in the nineteenth century.

It is, however, necessary, in assessing O'Connell's place in Irish history, to remember the actual limitations within which he had to work. It is true that he could bring great popular pressure to bear on government, but it must also be remembered that the political and economic influence of the landed ascendancy was very considerable and often very effective. We know, too, that throughout his career, O'Connell found it difficult to keep campaigns going over long periods, as public enthusiasm tended to flag. Again, it was no easy task to build up a coherent and disciplined party in Parliament at a time when members were unpaid and were inclined to look to government patronage for their reward. On another level, he had to contend with the fact that while many public men in Britain had actively sympathised with the cause of Catholic Emancipation, there was no significant support to be found inside or outside Parliament for Repeal.

Practical considerations, then, encouraged O'Connell to make compromises, to modify and, if necessary, to discard policies particularly when he believed that he could win some concessions from government. The unsuccessful attempts to bring the question of Repeal before Parliament, in 1834, for example, were quickly followed by his virtual abandonment of Repeal between 1835 and 1840. It was replaced by a policy of cooperation with the Whig ministry of Lord Melbourne. It needed the prospect of the return to office of his old Tory enemy, Sir Robert Peel, to swing O'Connell back to the Repeal cause in 1840.

Though the demand for a repeal of the Act of Union kept reasserting itself throughout his long career, the issue seldom assumed for O'Connell an absolute or rigid character and the exact implications of Repeal, in constitutional and administrative terms, remained very ill-defined. He put his rather pragmatic position well, in 1840, when he said: "If we get the justice we require, then our Repeal Association is at an end, but I know we will not get that justice".[3] His nationalism owed relatively little to those new ideas about the nation and its characteristics which had become popular in radical circles on the continent in the decades following the French Revolution. He would have been more at home with the constitutional principles of the eighteenth-century Patriot Party in the Irish Parliament.

O'Connell, however, was not afraid of controversy outside of the polite conventions of Parliament. His language on the platform could have a revolutionary quality about it and the threat he represented to the stability of government in Ireland was, at times, considered sufficiently menacing to seriously trouble British administrations. This was especially evident in 1843, when the rapid spread and popularity of the Repeal agitation caused great alarm in official circles in both Dublin and London. The agitation, built around the "Monster Meetings", was to collapse when the Clontarf meeting was proclaimed in October, but in the spring and summer men as experienced as Peel and his Home Secretary, Sir James Graham, considered that they had very good reasons to be concerned about Irish affairs and, in particular, O'Connell's bold claim that Repeal could be gained in 1843.

The years 1842 and 1843 were difficult times in Britain. By the summer of 1843, tne Anti-Corn Law campaign had won a great deal of support, the Rebecca riots in Wales were a disturbing symptom of working-class discontent as were the continuing activities of the Chartists. There was always the danger that British and Irish radicals would join forces. John Bright, the radical, warned the government of the urgent need for reforms, after his victory in a Durham by-election, "with insurrection threatening them more or less near, in Ireland, in Wales and in the north of England"[4]. Sir James Graham, discussing the risks involved in possibly having to proclaim the Repeal Association and the Anti-Corn Law League came to much the same conclusion when he told the Prime Minister: "if we attack both, we shall embark on a sea of trouble, and enter on a course of measures, which may precipitate disastrous events in both countries at the same time"[5]. Men of property were troubled, indeed, alarmed by the pattern of events in both Britain and Ireland.

A Repeal campaign was hardly likely to overthrow the Union in the short run, but O'Connell had reasonable grounds for believing that defiant language and strong actions could wring substantial concessions from Parliament. He gambled on winning, knowing how critical the situation was in Britain, but Sir Robert Peel, who had long regarded him as a dangerous demagogue and a threat to the British constitution, held the stronger cards and played them well. Before the end of 1843, the Repeal agitation had been effectively halted. Despite the fears and speculations, there was no real risk, we now know, of an organised rising in Ireland, though obviously the situation could have got out of control, given the nature of the agitation and its extent. No preparations had been made for a rebellion and O'Connell did not think in such terms. Even in the high excitement of the summer, O'Connell, the lawyer, was careful not to get too close to the brink of sedition or treason. He was resolved to avoid any entanglements with continental revolutionaries or even with the British Chartists. The fact that so little could be laid against him in the State Trials of 1844 is one measure of his ultimate caution.

Outside Ireland, especially among Catholic liberals in France, Germany and Italy, the O'Connellite movement was seen as a dramatic proof that liberal principles could be reconciled successfully with Catholic teachings. O'Connell had demonstrated that a liberal need not be anti-clerical or tainted by Jacobin or anti-monarchist influences. As Ventura, the Italian priest and political liberal, put it, Ireland had adopted "true liberty which is the daughter of religion"[6].

He saw this as O'Connell's great triumph. In the wider European context, therefore, O'Connell the liberal reformer tended to overshadow O'Connell the nationalist. An astute observer, the Italian nationalist and statesman, Camillo Cavour, could observe in this connection that the true reality behind O'Connell's political agitation was the well-justified demand for good government in Ireland and a better system of land tenure rather than national independence[7].

O'Connell's concern about reforms had, in fact, a wider dimension than the strictly Irish one. He opposed slavery, took a deep interest in the welfare of the peasants in India and was critical of the power exercised by the hereditary House of Lords. He campaigned against the privileged position of the Church of England, as an established church, and in this he shared common ground with many British radicals and non-conformists. Again, the cause of local government reform had for him an United Kingdom dimension. In the field of social change, he was usually cautious and he was no enemy of private property, but he did assert that the Irish tenant farmers should be given sufficient security of tenure to protect them against the landlords' exactions and evictions.

The success of the Catholic Emancipation campaign gave O'Connell a formidable source of popular support, but that campaign had also made it clear to Irish Protestants that the Catholic masses had, at last, become a potent political force. It would, however, be incorrect to conclude that O'Connell thought only in terms of the grievances and aspirations of the Catholic majority. His liberal principles and his debt to the Irish parliamentarians of the eighteenth century were reflected in his contention that, among Repealers, the question asked was "not to what religion a man belongs, but whether he is a true-born Irishman"[8]. He sought Protestant support for Repeal and he frequently stressed that he rejected any notion of a Catholic ascendancy under a restored Irish Parliament, yet he failed to discover a means of reconciling Protestant fears with Catholic hopes. In the circumstances, the Irish Catholics remained the basis of his power as they were to remain the source of popular backing for all subsequent nationalist movements, be they of a constitutional or a revolutionary kind.

It can be argued that it was a miscalculation on O'Connell's part to have placed so much emphasis on Catholic Emancipation rather than on repeal of the Union, in the years before 1829, if Protestant and landlord support were to be recruited. This would be to ignore the political realities of the time. Emancipation, for the reasons we have been considering, had the stronger appeal, not least in Britain, in the immediate post-Union situation, and O'Connell realised this. But the fact remains that, when the great Repeal campaign was launched in the eighteen-forties, the movement preserved an essentially Catholic character. Protestant supporters O'Connell had, and some of them were important, but the majority of their co-religionists remained suspicious or hostile to O'Connell and Repeal.

Though Repeal failed to become an all embracing political movement, it did ensure that Ireland's claim to some measure of political independence remained a serious political issue in the mid-nineteenth century. Any acceptance of a full identification with Great Britain was resisted on a wide, popular basis. Again, it was within the framework of the Repeal Association that a new kind of nationalism, at variance with many of O'Connell's assumptions and methods, began to take shape.

Among those who joined the ranks of the Association, between 1840 and 1843, were men such as Thomas Davis, Charles Gavan Duffy, John Blake Dillon and John Mitchel. They were the men of the *Nation* newspaper. These new recruits, it must be stressed, saw, as O'Connell did, the repeal of the Act of Union, and the restoration of legislative independence, as the great aim of their political endeavours. The nationalism of the Young Irelanders, as they came to be called, had a distinctive character of its own. Their frequent appeals to Irish history and legend, their emphasis on the importance of an integrated nationalism which would be cultural as well as political in its structure, brought them close to that romantic approach to nationalism which was so characteristic of the early nineteenth century in Germany, Italy, Bohemia and many other European lands. The nation had for them a unique identity and a spiritual value which could not be compromised. They would not forego national independence for any lesser concessions from government. To an even greater extent than did O'Connell, they hoped that the Repeal movement would win the support of all sections of the community, Catholic and Protestant, but they were to be no more successful than he had been.

O'Connell and the Young Irelanders, in the disappointing years between 1843 and 1846, when Peel had effectively halted the great

Repeal agitation, did not quarrel about the ultimate political objective. It remained, as before, parliamentary independence under the same Crown as Great Britain. The major area of dispute was, as we have seen, about the extent to which national claims could be subordinated to tactical considerations and immediate gains. This all had an urgency in view of the possibility of a new alliance between the Repealers and the English Whigs who were, of course, as much opposed to a repeal of the Act of Union as Peel and his supporters.

The tensions within the Repeal Association were highlighted, too, by a number of secondary issues, such as the way the Association was organised, the use of funds and by what the Young Irelanders considered to be vulgar, demagogic methods and excessive clerical influences. Thomas Davis, writing to William Smith O'Brien, could complain about "unaccounted funds, bigotry, Billingsgate... crude and contradictory dogmas and unrelieved stupidity..".[9] This crisis of confidence between Old and Young Ireland reached its climax, in the summer of 1846, during the debates in the Association on the abstract question of the possible use of physical force to achieve political ends. O'Connell proposed, to avoid any legal risks, that the Association should reassert its reliance on peaceful means alone, while his opponents argued that the interests of a nation might, sometime, necessitate a recourse to arms. The outcome was an open split, in 1846, between Old and Young Ireland and the two parties were not to be reunited in O'Connell's lifetime, though attempts at reconciliation were made.

Sir Robert Peel's resolute action, in 1843-4, the internal disputes within the Association and, above all, the agony of the Great Famine combined to bring about the rapid decline and dissolution of the Repeal movement. It survived the death of O'Connell, in May 1847, but only as a shadow and, by 1849, Repeal was no longer of political significance in Ireland. The Repeal movement had, however, made a substantial contribution to the shaping of an Irish political pattern. O'Connell, in the eighteen-twenties and again in the eighteen-forties, had shown how to organise and to use mass political pressure and in doing so had helped to bring the ordinary people into constitutional politics. This was liberalism being given effective expression on the ground. It was the beginnings of a democratic process.

The O'Connellite movement, despite the serious setbacks from

1843-4 onwards, provided the first effective expression of constitutional and moderate nationalism in nineteenth century Ireland. The goal, Repeal, may have lacked precision, but the agitation gave expression to the belief that an Irish political and legislative identity could be achieved while still retaining a special link with Great Britain in constitutional terms. O'Connell's way was based essentially on popular consent and the rejection of violence and yet, in a sense, the Repeal movement, through men like John Mitchel and Devin Reilly, the more radical of the Young Irelanders, had also helped to bring a separatist and republican factor into Irish politics, between 1847 and 1849. Their thinking, however, was not O'Connell's.

The legacy of Daniel O'Connell to Irish nationalism, was to be seen in the great Home Rule movement of the late nineteenth century, in many of the ideas of men like Arthur Griffith and in those compromises which made the Irish Free State possible and which, it can be argued, are still relevant to-day.

Notes

1. Daniel O'Connell to Maurice O'Connell, 23 (and 24) January 1797, Maurice R. O'Connell (ed.), *The correspondence of Daniel O'Connell*, i.30.
2. John O'Connell (ed.), *Select Speeches of Daniel O'Connell, M.P.*, i.215.
3. *Freeman's Journal*, 16 April 1840.
4. *Morning Chronicle*, 31 July 1843.
5. Graham to Peel, 7 May 1843, Peel Papers, B.M. Add.MS 40448,ff.297-300.
6. Gioacchino Ventura, *Funeral Oration on O'Connell*.
7. Camillo Cavour, *Thoughts on Ireland* (trans. W. B. Hodgson),p.41.
8. *Freeman's Journal*, 14 July 1840.
9. Thomas Davis to William Smith O'Brien, 26 July 1845, Smith O'Brien Papers, N.Lib.Ir., vol.435, no.1371.

2

The Changing Image of O'Connell

Donal McCartney

On his death-bed in Genoa in May 1847 Daniel O'Connell is alleged to have committed his soul to its Creator, his heart to Rome and his body to Ireland. This final testament proves, not what John Mitchel claimed, "how miserably broken and debilitated was that once potent nature",[1] but on the contrary, what a consummate politician O'Connell was even to the end. For with so august a trinity on his side—God, Rome and Ireland—O'Connell could hardly lose, certainly not in the years immediately following his death.

Not even the shrewdest politician, however, can order the image of himself that he would wish to pass on down through history. Men of later generations insist on portraying their heroes and their villains according to the needs of their own times. So the role played by O'Connell as legend was different in many respects from the actual role he played in his own lifetime.

The legend has varied with the times. And the assessments that have been made of his career serve as a barometer measuring Ireland's political atmosphere over the last century and a quarter. During that time, Irish moods, dreams, aspirations, doubts and anxieties were all reflected in the various images of O'Connell created and invoked. "Tell me your opinion of O'Connell and I'll tell you what kind of patriot you are" is a test that could be made of any generation of Irish nationalists. No one could talk or write about O'Connell without giving away something of his own political attitudes and beliefs.

The legend began in O'Connell's own lifetime, for he was both the most idolized and the best hated public man of his time. To millions of Irish peasants, he was their Uncrowned King. To *The Times* of London he was:

> Scum condensed of Irish bog,
> Ruffian, coward, Demagogue.[2]

A contemporary, D. O. Maddyn wrote:

He is a saint and a miscreant—a coward and a hero—a ranter and a genius—a trafficking demagogue and a mighty statesman—a base hypocrite and an honest politician; all according to the prejudices of those who pronounce judgment on him.[3]

Most of the adverse criticism of O'Connell was drowned—momentarily at any rate—in the flood of adulation that accompanied him to the grave. Pius IX, receiving the bearers of the heart, called O'Connell, "the great champion of the Church, the father of his country, the glory of the Christian world".[4] And taking their cue from the Pope, grateful churchmen in Ireland, loyal colleagues and close family lauded O'Connell's greatness in the years that followed his death, and propagated the cult of O'Connellism based on the integrated theme of Faith and Fatherland. In the generation between his death in 1847 and the death of Cardinal Paul Cullen in 1878, O'Connell was pictured primarily in the role of Liberator—the Liberator of the Irish Catholics. It was in the Church that Paul Cullen built in Ireland that O'Connell was, so to speak, "Cullenized". A proud, aggressive but also narrow and defensive Irish Catholicism captured the legend and O'Connell looked in his Liberator's mantle much less liberal than, in fact, he had been during his public career. In the 1850's, particularly in the hey-day of the Catholic Defence Association, the Independent Irish Party and Tenant Right, O'Connell's massive frame was reduced to make him fit the role of a shrunken mascot of the Pope's Brass Band. In the 1860's, he was used as a weapon with which to beat the Fenians, the Orangemen, and the Established Church. In August 1864, Archbishops and Bishops marched in the procession that marked the laying of the foundation stone of a national memorial to O'Connell at the end of what was then Sackville Street. But in Belfast, that same August, O'Connell was burned in effigy by an Orange mob, thus sparking off sectarian riots which only ended after seven people had been killed and 150 others seriously injured.

In the 1870's, O'Connell was even being used as a weapon against Home Rule by those who, like the Catholic Lord Mayor, Peter Paul MacSwiney, and the Cardinal, Paul Cullen, regarded the early Home Rule movement as a dangerous conspiracy thought up by political economists of TCD and other bigoted Orangemen. For Cullen's political hero was O'Connell the Liberator, if not O'Connell the Repealer or O'Connell the radical reformer. It is significant that, among the two most popular works on O'Connell written during this period, one was written by a priest, and the other by a nun.[5]

And so the cult of O'Connell in the first thirty years after his death was strictly Constitutional but also aggressively Catholic. By capturing him for their own party ends, these rather pious early chroniclers and admirers of his career had done him less than justice. And by shaping him into a kind of political goodie-goodie smelling of incense and candles, they had canonised the old rascal, created misunderstanding of his real contribution to Irish history and made deadly enemies for him among some of the more independent and intelligent young nationalists of the day. With friends such as he had, it might well be asked, did he need enemies? But O'Connell's enemies were massing their forces for a powerful counter-attack.

Unfortunately, for O'Connell's reputation, he had found himself during his last years opposed by one of the most talented groups of young men ever to combine in Irish politics—the Young Irelanders. Two of these in particular—John Mitchel and Charles Gavan Duffy—were not only extremely gifted writers and propagandists, but were eventually to devote a vast amount of their talent, energy, and time to the utter demolition of the O'Connell myth. If this two-pronged attack had been long-thought-out and co-ordinated, it could not have been more effective than it was. O'Connell, revisited many years after his death by Mitchel and then Duffy, was to suffer at their hands a severe diminution of whatever stature the would-be friends had left him.

The final break between O'Connell and Young Ireland had taken place in July 1846 on the issue of moral as opposed to physical force. The so-called Peace Resolutions had stated the Repeal Association sought its objectives by peaceable and legal means *alone*, and disclaimed *all* attempts to win constitutional liberty by force, violence and bloodshed. The Young Irelanders chose to interpret the Resolutions as implying that in no circumstances was force ever justifiable, although the Resolutions had specifically allowed the use of self-defence against aggression. In a letter (21 Nov. 1846) to Michael Blake, Bishop of Dromore, O'Connell explained the difference between himself and the seceders. His position, as always, was that repeal should be carried by "peaceable, legal and constitutional means and by *none other*". The seceders, he said, insisted that in the event of peaceable and legal means failing then they should reserve to themselves "the use in any favourable opportunity of the sword". O'Connell however was not prepared to sacrifice the principle of non-violence and risk putting in jeopardy the liberties and lives of members of the Association. The debate was academic in the sense that no side advocated force in the circumstances. And read soberly today, one of the odd things about the debate is that we have on the one hand the "party of the sword" professing the most peaceful intentions but clinging to their dogma that force wasn't everywhere and always wrong, confronted by the advocate of exclusively constitutional action, admitting that under certain contingencies the use of physical resistance might be justified. In the end, the metaphysicians, Mitchel, Duffy and their friends walked out of Conciliation Hall and the Repeal Association. Mitchel, later arrested for treason-felony, was sentenced to fourteen years transportation but escaped after a few years to America.

After his escape, his writings became extremely influential in the development of Irish nationalism. For Pearse, he was one of the four evangelists of Irish nationalism. For Arthur Griffith, no country had a nobler or more gallant figure in its pantheon. His books, all written with tremendous force, preached Republicanism pure and simple and the use of arms to achieve the Independent Republic. Throughout all his sermons, this perhaps most eloquent of the holy-haters of England in the Irish nationalist tradition, delivered many a savage side-blow at his former leader in the Repeal movement. In Mitchel's searing words O'Connell was: "Next to the British Government, the worst enemy that Ireland ever had, or rather the most fatal friend".[6]

Mitchel was greatly impressed by the hold which O'Connell had over the people—whether, as he said, "by a kind of divine or else diabolic right". But, he believed that O'Connell had led them all wrong for forty years. O'Connell's "finest peasantry in the world", said Mitchel, were by no means a stupid race. But the magician bewitched them to their utter destruction. Mitchel's pen-picture of the contradictions in that magician's character will bear repeating for many a day yet:

> Poor old Dan, wonderful, mighty, jovial, and mean old man with silver tongue and smile of witchery, and heart of melting ruth—lying tongue, smile of treachery, heart of unfathomable fraud! What a royal yet vulgar soul, with the keen eye and potent swoop of a generous eagle of Cairn Tual—with the base servility of a hound

and the cold cruelty of a spider! Think of his speech for John Magee, the most powerful forensic achievement since before Demosthenes—and think of the 'gorgeous and gossamer' theory of moral and peaceful agitation, the most astounding *organon* of public swindling since first man bethought him of obtaining money under false pretences. And after one has thought of all this, and more, what then can a man *say*? What but pray that Irish earth may lie light on O'Connell's breast—and that the Good God who knew how to create so wondrous a creature may have mercy upon his soul.[7]

O'Connell's greatest treachery, in the eyes of Mitchel, was that he had called off the Clontarf Monster Meeting in October 1843 because the Government had banned it at the last moment and threatened force against all who tried to assemble. Mitchel agreed that if the troops had fired on the people there would have been a horrible slaughter of the unarmed peasantry and O'Connell himself might have fallen. "It were well for his reputation if he had," added Mitchel. And the death of five or ten thousand people at Clontarf might have saved Ireland the slaughter by famine of one hundred times as many shortly afterwards. This stunning assertion was repeated by Mitchel both in the *History of Ireland* and in *The Last Conquest*. But, of course, he was never to explain how a massacre at Clontarf in '43 could have averted the slaughter by Famine which began in '45. Mitchel, however had become utterly convinced that Irish liberty could only be earned by the sword, and that lesson was the burden of all his writing after 1847. In his *Jail Journal*, he faced up to his own question: did he, then, desire to plunge his country into a deluge of slaughter. And he answered that question frankly: "I prescribe copious blood-letting upon strictly therapeautical principles."[8] It was this kind of remark which inspired the young Lecky (then a student in TCD but already planning an essay which would be one of the most penetrating and judicious examinations of O'Connell) to confide to his note-book under the heading of "J. Mitchel and Co."—"There are some quack doctors who have but one remedy—bleeding."[9]

Mitchel's onslaught on O'Connell was very damaging both to O'Connell's reputation and to the policies which he had advocated. For Mitchel's views not only represented, but also influenced, some of the more idealistic nationalists who came after him. It was, nevertheless, a frontal attack, direct and obvious, and therefore not particularly calculated to destroy O'Connell's standing with the more moderate or constitutional nationalists. But the vast credit which O'Connell had accumulated among the constitutionalists was now to be undermined by the far more subtle and insidious methods of Gavan Duffy.

Duffy, after nine months imprisonment, had been acquitted in 1849. He returned to edit *The Nation*, but in 1855 he quitted what he called "the blind and bitter land", for he could not live in a country where, he said, Keogh and Sadlier typified patriotism and Dr. Cullen typified the Church. In Australia he was eventually to become Prime Minister of Victoria. He returned to live in Europe in 1880 and from then until his death in 1903, volumes of historical comment poured from his pen.[10]

More than any other writer, Duffy was responsible for the "de-O'Connellization" of Irish history. And this he did largely by a process that might be called the "Davisization" of Irish nationalism. He raised his friend of the early 1840's, Thomas Davis, into a giant, beside whose political purity, goodness and wisdom O'Connell seemed vulgar and dwarfish. After Duffy was finished with the period, which he made very much his own, O'Connell's portrait could never be seen again without a search for serious blemishes in his character and politics. Mitchel's sketch of O'Connell had been strictly for the converted: his fervid phrases could be used as an armoury for Fenians, Fenian sympathisers and their successors. But Duffy's picture of O'Connell, written in a prose that was as sober as Mitchel's was high-pitched, was calculated to win converts, to sow doubts in the minds of O'Connell's glorifiers and to drive them on to the defensive. The pen Duffy used was dipped in a more subtle poison than Mitchel's. The Duffy portrait was ingenious, factually impressive, and studiously moderate, but all the more devastating for that.

Duffy in the 1880's and 90's looked exactly like the honest, impartial and elder statesman that he claimed to be in his writings. He said that whatever was rash or ungenerous in his earlier judgements he had revised, and had striven to be accurate, fair and temperate. His credentials were unquestionable: he had, as he said, no longer anything to ask or fear from fortune. And he had tried to be as scrupulously just as if he were engaged on a Last Confession.

It was the apparent moderation in Duffy's tone that proved most effective in his demolition of O'Connell. The generosity of his praise for O'Connell in the Emancipation struggle entitled him to criticise

O'Connell's handling of Repeal. O'Connell's just fame and affection-
ate remembrance in Ireland, said Duffy, guaranteed a favourable
interpretation whenever O'Connell's controversies with others were
examined. But it should not be forgotten that the young men who had
opposed him, and who now were scattered all over the world, had
everywhere proved themselves men of honour and ability and therefore
entitled to be heard even against O'Connell. Duffy's ability made
certain that *they* got their hearing. O'Connell was less fortunate with
his counsel for the defence.

And so, the picture slowly, skilfully and imperceptibly emerged of
the Young Irelanders as young men of principle opposed by an old,
scheming, jealous, self-centred, unscrupulous, overbearing, untruthful,
rapacious politician. O'Connell was only half the patriot with half the
talent of his former self. The reason, according to Duffy, was old age, a
generation gap and the deadly influence of that villain of the piece,
O'Connell's son John. By blaming old age and son John rather than
O'Connell himself, Duffy was allowing admirers of O'Connell to
accept this censure without giving them the feeling that they were
deserting their hero. He made a lot out of this point of O'Connell's age
and returned to it time and time again (in this connection it is not un-
important to remember that when O'Connell retreated from Clontarf
he was exactly one year older than Duffy was when the latter criticised
him in his *Four Years of Irish History* (1883). It was the case of a man
of 67 claiming that a man of 68 was too old to have any political sense
left in his body).

Duffy's Young Ireland friends were made to appear as martyrs,
O'Connell's political friends as place-hunters. In the 1830's, said Duffy,
O'Connell abandoned self-government for good government and equal
justice. Several Repealers accepted appointments under the system
they had recently been pledged to overthrow. This acceptance of office,
admitted Duffy, did not outrage public opinion, as it would have done
at a later period. The admission, superficially just to O'Connell, at the
same time managed to suggest that not only had O'Connell got jobs
for the boys in his own time but had also spawned those placehunters
of Duffy's time, Sadlier and Keogh, and all their ilk.

O'Connell had co-operated with the Whig Government in the 1830's
to the extent of not embarrassing them with demands for Repeal as
long as they attempted the better government of Ireland. He had toyed

with the same idea in the last year of his career. Young Ireland disapproved of this Whig Alliance as they had also disapproved of the hand he had held out to the Federalists, and Duffy's comments on these matters made O'Connell's political pragmatism seem like deviation from the principle of independence to which he had pleged himself and his people. And the criticism lost none of its effect despite the odd circumstance that it was made by a moderate constitutionalist who had been knighted for his services to the British Empire. O'Connell at least, had always remained plain Daniel, while his very skilful critic had meanwhile become Sir Charles.

Duffy was no rebel and no brash advocate of bloodshed. Yet his criticism of O'Connell's retreat from Clontarf gave powerful backing to the Mitchel thesis. He selected every note of defiance that O'Connell had spoken before Clontarf and implied that O'Connell had pledged himself to fight should the government ban his meeting. Duffy's case was that O'Connell had failed to carry out what he had threatened. Yet, it was not as clear-cut a moral issue as Duffy made it. Had O'Connell fought and failed, asked Duffy, could the result have been more disastrous? And he went on to point out that more had been slaughtered in the Famine than had fallen in three French Revolutions; and more had been exiled by political despair than had been banished from France under the tyranny of Louis XIV. This was Duffy's indirect way of supporting Mitchel's thesis that bloodletting at Clontarf would in some mysterious way have staved off the Famine. Adroitly Duffy had managed to hold O'Connell responsible for the millions who had died either in the Famine or who had gone out as exiles from the despairing land.

O'Connell should have backed up his demands with armed Volunteers, said Duffy, and then in some future crisis the British Government would have capitulated as they had done to Grattan in 1782. This lesson was taken up very seriously by the Irish Volunteers in 1913. But Eoin MacNeill and Arthur Griffith and other admirers of Duffy's plan overlooked, as had Duffy himself, that ardent spirits in arms cannot always be controlled by arguments about maintaining a defensive posture, especially if a Government should show no disposition to yield, and the prospects for rebellion seem bright. Those men like Mitchel, or later Pearse, who advocated direct offensive rebellion, had at least the merit of carrying the argument of arms to its logical conclusion.

By 1900, then, O'Connell who had been Catholicised by his admirers had been de-nationalised by his enemies. Duffy, however powerful his influence on the nationalist interpretation of O'Connell, had in a sense only confirmed with chapter and verse opinions already making headway. A. M. Sullivan, a constitutionalist opposed to Fenianism, and one of the great propagandists of Home Rule, also faulted O'Connell's behaviour at Clontarf. Sullivan's *Story of Ireland*, "written for the youth of Ireland", a very popular work in the late 19th century, described O'Connell's conviction about the efficacy of moral force as "the gigantic error of his life".[11] Sullivan was typical of those many constitutionalists who compensated for their rich abuse of contemporary Fenianism and physical force by glorifying every manifestation of arms and rebellion in the past. Because of the paradox in Irish nationalism which transformed contemporary moderates into rebels in their historical sympathies, Home Rulers who might have been expected to have regarded O'Connell as their hero, in large measure disowned him.

In the intense flame of Irish nationalism between 1900 and 1922 O'Connell was less likely than ever to be restored to the favour of his countrymen. The historical dice had been loaded too heavily against him. For in the first place the constitutional Home Rulers had little time for him. But even more seriously for his reputation, supporters of the Gaelic Revival, Sinn Feiners, Socialists and Republicans were inclined to accept the Mitchel view that it were better for Ireland had O'Connell never been born. The men of the Gaelic Revival argued that because O'Connell was a political giant he had done more than any other man to kill the language, and the distinctive character of the nation. For Griffith and his Sinn Féin friends O'Connell was the father of lies who had invented that great evil, Parliamentarianism, the policy of trying to redress Ireland's grievances in the English Parliament which by itself, said Griffith, had done nothing except turn the eyes of the people away from Ireland and themselves. The one fleeting moment of truth in O'Connell's career, according to Griffith, was when he had spoken of withdrawing from Westminster and establishing a Council of 300 in Ireland. James Connolly described O'Connell as the bitterest enemy of the Irish working class and their trade unions. O'Connell was banned from Pearse's pantheon because, said Pearse, he had taught no doctrine except the obviously untrue one that liberty was too dearly purchased at the price of a single drop of blood. Even the scholarly

Eoin MacNeill labelled O'Connell as "the ultra constitutionalist", guilty of the error of imagining that the power of constitutional agitation was irresistible. And an *Irish History Reader* by the Christian Brothers, popular in the early twentieth century, confessed that it was a strange weakness of O'Connell to imagine for a moment that cheers and speeches could force the British nation to loose its hold on Ireland. O'Connell's failure to win Repeal and the failure of his 'moral force' policy helped to make rebels out of his successors.

All in all, then, from 1848 to 1922 it had been a very strong line-out against O'Connell—every influential newspaper and almost every first rank propagandist in the nationalist camp, and every popular history text book made its contribution to the demolition of the man and his politics. Nor have the echoes of these denunciations died out yet. Among others the late Earnán de Blaghad was very fond of blaming O'Connell not only for the decline of the language, but even for the partition of the country. In an Ireland that approved of force for the attainment of political objectives it had become fashionable to attribute all our ills to this champion of non-violence. For O'Connell was the nearest thing to a convinced pacifist that Irish history ever produced. Our failures and our faults were all reflected in our image of O'Connell. He had become the great national scapegoat, dishonoured and misunderstood as much by his friends as by his enemies.

When O'Connell was revisited after the trauma of the Civil War, however, the portrait at last began to change. P. S. O'Hegarty, for example, who earlier had shared many of Griffith's views about O'Connell, had been on the Supreme Council of the IRB, and had sided with Griffith and Collins on the Treaty, took a much more benign view of O'Connell in his *History of Ireland under the Union* (1952). O'Hegarty was now equipped with bitter personal experience of the difficulties which Griffith and Collins had faced in the opposition of the doctrinaire Republicans. O'Hegarty, therefore, found it easier to appreciate O'Connell's position in his quarrels with the young doctrinaire militants of 1846. Sean O Faoláin had also come to write his brilliant biography of O'Connell, *King of the Beggars*, with the experience of the Civil War behind him. Ó Faoláin had taken the anti-Treaty side but when de Valera entered the Dáil in 1927 he complained that de Valera's explanation as to whether he had taken the Oath made him "squirm". He approached O'Connell as "the greatest of all Irish realists".[12] What he called the "righteous self-belief"[13] of de Valera was contrasted unfavourably with O'Connell's political realism.

O'Connell (or Collins), said Ó Faoláin, would have come out of the Oath situation if not as angels, certainly as men. Michael Tierney, too, in his *Daniel O'Connell: Nine Century Essays* (1948) also glorified O'Connell, the realist—the Christian realist—he called him, the very antithesis of Pearse and his pagan blood sacrifice mystique. And Tierney, too, coupled the name of O'Connell with that of Collins. Strange bed-fellows these, O'Connell and Collins—you might well say. But to Tierney, Collins had been foreshadowed by O'Connell. They were the two grand opportunists of political action in Irish history. O'Connell, he said, had Collins' penetrating grasp of a military situation, while the military tactics employed by Collins were in reality those of O'Connell's passive resistance campaigns only differently applied. The work of Professor Denis Gwynn also gave strong support to this post-Civil War revision. And more recently the work of academic historians, by inducing us to judge O'Connell in his own time, has also tended to restore the stature of O'Connell. Despite the survival of strong critical reverberations an image of O'Connell which the peasantry of his own time would readily recognise has been in the process of restoration since 1922. And the Angel of one group of propagandists and the Demon of another have been replaced by an historical figure with more human proportions.

O'Connell, therefore has been to Irish historiography what Napoleon is to French. He is an argument without end. He has been, and remains, the touchstone of Irish political attitudes. When we Catholicized him we were as a people pious and devotional. When we condemned his retreat from Clontarf and his moral force doctrine we were in militant, nationalistic mood. When we wrote him off as a mere politician and pragmatist we were doctrinaires and idealists. And what we omitted to say about O'Connell in the last century and a quarter was as much tell-tale evidence against ourselves as what in fact we did say. We had concentrated largely on the twin peaks of his agitation, Emancipation and Repeal. The valley years in between (1830–40), when O'Connell was the Parliamentarian *par excellence*, have been generally ignored. The title of the chapter devoted to this period in one laudatory biography is called—significantly—"Ploughing the sands".[14] O'Connell as a European figure introducing French Revolutionary ideas of Liberty and Democracy without French Revolutionary Republicanism or Violence is also noticeable by its almost total absence from the consideration given to O'Connell in a nationalist age.

But, however one looks at O'Connell, he was obviously a big man inspiring both worship and antipathy. The Irish, said Churchill in a youthful essay, have always demanded Old Testament prophets in their political leaders. In that sense O'Connell was the Moses of Irish politics. By the stimulants of his oratory, his nation-wide organizing, his popular agitation, his passive resistance and civil disobedience, he was the man who set the pulse of his people racing—racing so fast, in fact, that within a relatively short period the position from which he himself had operated seemed to have been left a great distance behind in a land of Egypt, and light years away from that early twentieth-century world of Republicanism, Separatism, Socialism, Gaelic Revival and Blood Sacrifice. The very speed at which nineteenth-century Irish nationalism travelled away from O'Connell was, paradoxically, O'Connell's biggest contribution to Irish history.

And so, the debate goes on. Modern academic historians with much more of the source material available to them try to understand him rather than use him for propaganda purposes. Nevertheless among the academics O'Connell has his admirers and apologists as well as critics—as anyone dipping into their work can readily perceive. We can be sure that out of the Northern Ireland situation of Civil Rights, Violence and Power-sharing, O'Connell's civil rights campaign in the Emancipation struggle, his doctrine of non-violence that one live patriot was worth a whole graveyard of dead ones, and his power-sharing in the Whig Alliance, will take on newer meaning. And O'Connell, revisited, in these circumstances will tell us whether we as a people are clinging to old ways and old modes of thought or whether we have broken new ground in Irish political attitudes and thinking by returning to re-examine his methods and objectives.

For O'Connell was and is a man for all Irish political seasons. Delivering O'Connell's funeral oration in Rome, Ventura said: "God does not create a great man for the use of a single age or a single people".[15] O'Connell's continuing career as a legend has justified his claim to greatness as a man, a man moreover who is well-worth revisiting in the current crisis of Ireland's political odyssey.

Notes

1. John Mitchel, *Jail Journal* (1913 edition), pp. xl–xli.
2. *The Times*, 26 Nov. 1835.
3. D. O. Maddyn, *Ireland and its rulers: since 1829* (3 vols, 1844), I, p. 12.
4. Michael MacDonagh, *Daniel O'Connell and the story of Catholic Emancipation* (1929), p. 374.
5. Very Rev. Canon John O'Rourke, The Centenary Life of O'Connell (7th edn., 1900); Mary F. Cusack, *The Liberator: his life and times, political, social and religious* (1872).
6. John Mitchel, *The last conquest of Ireland (perhaps)* (n.d.), p. 136.
7. John Mitchel, *Jail Journal*, p. 141.
8. John Mitchel, Ibid., p. 92.
9. Trinity College Dublin, MS R.7.30, p. 72.
10. Charles Gavan Duffy, *Young Ireland: a fragment of Irish history, 1840–1845* (1880); *Young Ireland, Part II or Four Years of Irish History 1845–1849* (1883); *The League of North and South* (1886); *Thomas Davis: the memoires of an Irish patriot 1840–1846* (1890); *My life in two hemispheres* (2 vols, 1898).
11. A. M. Sullivan, *The story of Ireland* (n.d.), p. 552.
12. S. ÓFaoláin, *King of the Beggars* (1938), p. 368.
13. S. ÓFaoláin, *De Valera* (Penguin, 1939), p. 123.
14. D. Gwynn, *Daniel O'Connell* (1929, Revised edn. 1947).
15. Quoted in J. J. O'Kelly, *O'Connell calling* (1847), p. 144. A translation of Ventura's oration is given in William B. MacCabe, *The last days of O'Connell* (1847), pp. 121–200.

3

O'Connell and the Gaelic World

John A. Murphy

Historians have come to stress O'Connell's significance as British parliamentarian and European liberal in addition, of course, to his major, and long-accepted, role as Irish "Liberator". Yet if we are to comprehend the fullness of his personality we need to investigate another dimension. He was a native speaker of Irish who constantly returned to his deep Kerry roots. How did this basic fact influence him? How did he see the Gaelic world of his time? How did that world see him? What was his attitude to the linguistic and cultural changes which gathered pace during his lifetime? Was he himself a significant agent of change in this process?

We now know more about the Irish-speaking world of the 1820s than we did when the late Professor Gerard Murphy treated in 1947 of O'Connell's Gaelic background.[1] Recent research has shown that Irish was still used to a surprising extent as a political medium in the great debates of the day—Emancipation, anti-Tithe and Repeal. Of course, English was the vehicle of the politicisation of the Catholic masses but Irish played a minor role as the language of response, so to speak. Moreover, the political and social ideas we find in the Irish language sources are frequently different *in kind*: O'Connellism, as we shall see, was interpreted by the remaining heirs of the Gaelic tradition to their own taste.

Irish-speaking Ireland in the early nineteenth century continued to contract.[2] For a long period Irish had been a hunted language, its scholarship gradually declining, thrown back introspectively on itself. For two or three centuries, English had been the language of government, law, business and politics and, more recently, the language which expressed Catholic aspirations to equality and Irish aspirations to independence. It was rapidly becoming the dominant language of the pulpit. It was, moreover, for individual Irishmen the indispensable language of *advance*. Nevertheless, throughout O'Connell's lifetime,

Irish was the language of *life* for great masses of Irishmen: for precisely how many it is impossible to say. Pro- and anti-Irish language lobbyists stretch what evidence there is to suit their conflicting purposes. Before the 1851 Census the evidence on the subject is scanty, and even when statistics begin to be recorded their reliability is highly questionable for various reasons. However, we can reasonably surmise that in the exciting prime of O'Connell's career Irish was the everyday language of at least two and a half million people, though the number of monoglots among these continued to dwindle. Still, as the population soared to its pre-Famine peak, Irish was spoken by more people, in absolute terms, than ever before. But—and it is a very important qualification— there was both a geographical and social imbalance in the speaking of Irish: though it might still be heard in a few eastern districts such as Louth and Kilkenny, Gaelic Ireland was in the main the area west of the Cork–Derry axis. Even more significantly, Irish was the language of the *coismhuintir*, the *choitiantacht*:* it had long ceased to be spoken by Catholic merchants and gentry, by those who had managed to retain some wealth and position as well as by those who had political, social and economic aspirations. In the Liberator's time, the O'Connells of Derrynane would speak Irish, of course, to their inferiors: it is doubtful if they spoke it much among themselves.[3] And they corresponded exclusively in English. As for the ordinary people, a large and increasing majority—again what precise percentage it is impossible to say—were acquainted with English. One final point should be made about the Irish language in the early nineteenth century. Even before the institution of the National School system in 1831, there was little formal teaching of Irish: according to the First Report of the Commissioners of Irish Education Enquiry[4] only twenty-eight schools in all of Cork and Kerry taught Irish. In an age when illiteracy was the norm, very few Irishmen could read or write their ancestral language, though this point was a matter of contemporary argument.[5]

O'Connell's Gaelic background was Uibh Rathach (Iveragh), the mountainous and scenic peninsula that lies between Dingle Bay and Kenmare bay. In its time it was the largest and most intensive Irish-speaking area in Munster.[6] What cannot be stressed too strongly is O'Connell's deep and life-long attachment to this district—not only to his native Carhen and his beloved Derrynane but to the whole penin-

---

* The ordinary people, the commonalty. (All translations in the text and footnotes are my own).

sula. When he rejected a government offer of a chief judgeship, he reflected, half in jest, that it would have given him the opportunity to spend all the time he liked in Derrynane.[7] "Next to you and my babes", he wrote his wife, "I love Iveragh".[8] He told Walter Savage Landor how deeply its beauty affected him as a boy and stimulated his patriotic dreams.[9] More practically, he returned to Iveragh to hunt and shoot whenever he had the opportunity. Throughout his life, he found relaxation and recreation there, away from the pressures of politics and the law. Sometimes he stayed much longer than he intended, even breaking the pattern of frequent letter-writing to his wife: her reproach was muted by understanding ("I know how much you enjoy yourself always in Iveragh").[10] The "gratifying" pleasures of Kerry[11] sometimes included dancing "country dances as well as I used to do before I married".[12] But there was more to all this than mere vacationing: it was a return to roots, a constant nourishing of his *dúchas*,* a major element in his greatness. We find him several years in succession[13] making for home around 29 September for the traditional pattern day at Carhen. Thus in 1814 (when he was nearly forty) there were hunts and races on the strand "and I spent the rest of the day in deciding wrangles, preventing riots, throwing boys into the trenches and flinging hats among the crowds, etc".[14] Clearly, he still possessed that exuberance which had prompted his uncle's exasperated description of him twenty years earlier: "He is, I am told, employed in visiting the seats of hares at Keelrelig, the earths of foxes at Tarmons, the caves of otters at Bolus, and the celebration of Miss Burke's wedding at Direen...".[15] And always there were the teeming crowds, "my Kerry mobs",[16] as at the traditional wake and funeral of his father, Morgan, in 1809.[17]

The Gaelic world into which O'Connell was born was, first of all, extremely remote[18]—remote, that is, from Dublin and London. Iveragh was the centre of its own world: if it looked beyond itself at all, it was to Europe or more precisely to France. The Church and soldiering and smuggling were the links that bound Kerry to the Continent. As in so much else, O'Connell's life was an age of transition in this respect: the era of the Wild Geese ended as he grew up and this is personified in his uncle, the celebrated Count O'Connell. The whole Gaelic–Gallic world of these O'Connells is evocatively caught in Mrs. M. J. O'Connell's

* Hereditary nature or personality.

invaluable *Last Colonel of the Irish Brigade*.[19]

For the O'Connells as for the lower orders, at different levels, survival was the name of the game. Muiris an Chaipín, "Hunting-Cap", would have understood what Americans mean by the phrase "survival kit". The compromise and flexibility essential for survival left little room for ideology. This kind of mentality characterised the nephew as well as the uncle. Again, we must think of Uibh Rathach as a Gaeltacht* and of Daniel O'Connell as a Gaeltacht man. This is the key to much of his personality and behaviour. Gaeltacht people were, and are, pragmatic, adaptable, non- or even anti-republican and entirely without sentimentality about their language and way of life. Resourcefulness is a vital aspect of survival: *is cuma nó muc fear gan seift* is a highly significant proverb, "the man without stratagem is no better than a pig". Of course, this kind of resourcefulness had a literal application to the survival conditions of the *coitiantacht*† in the elemental world of the western sea-board, but it is not too fanciful to extend it to other dimensions of living. O'Connell all his life long demonstrated, of necessity, the survival instinct and there was no end to the flexibility and resourcefulness he displayed in the law courts, at the hustings and in parliament. In all this, he was the Gaeltacht man, *par excellence*.

There were other aspects of the Gaeltacht tradition which further illuminate O'Connell for us. The life-style at Derrynane was still patriarchal, familial and lavish. As host there in his later years O'Connell played a traditional role. Excessive drinking apart (to which he was temperamentally averse and which, as an ally of Fr. Mathew, he rejected[20]) he kept the style of the Gaelic Big House that his aunt, Eibhlín Dubh, so graphically describes in her *Caoineadh Airt Uí Laoghaire*.‡ The traveller, William Hewitt, visiting Derrynane a year and a half before the Counsellor's death (significantly, O'Connell was the "Counsellor" rather than the "Liberator" to his own people) was reminded forcefully of a Walter Scott-type Gaelic chieftain.[21] All through O'Connell's life, the ramifications of his vast family network were inescapable. The demands of his relatives on his legal expertise,[22] his money and his political patronage were incessant. To secure jobs for his relatives was what was naturally expected of him and of many an Irish political boss thereafter. So too with the never-repaid loans,

---

* A district where Irish is spoken as the native language.
† The common people.
‡ Lament for Art Ó Laoghaire.

the hospitality, the prodigality. All this led to a perpetual financial crisis which has been investigated by Professor Maurice O'Connell under the heading "Income, expenditure and despair".[23] O'Connell's chronic inability to manage his finances has various explanations, but we must not underrate the fact that he sprang from a tradition which judged a man's greatness by his hospitality and by his readiness to spend lavishly, regardless of the consequences.

According to the canons of the nationalism that became the later orthodoxy, Daniel O'Connell was the great West Briton of the nineteenth century, explicitly and deliberately rejecting his priceless cultural heritage for the English fleshpots. That stern moralist of the Irish cultural revolution, Daniel Corkery, speaks about O'Connell's "callousness" and the "harm" done by him, and castigates his "disastrous (legal) type of mind".[24] Even such admiring biographers as "Sceilg", Fr. Antoine Ó Duibhir and Domhnall Ó Suilleabháin either reproach him for not having been a language enthusiast or feel they must really explain anew what they believe to have been his attitude to Irish. "Sceilg", indeed, clearly refuses to believe in his indifference to the language.[25]

What in fact did the Irish language mean to O'Connell? He imbibed it with his foster-mother's milk, and it remained part and parcel of him thereafter. This is not readily evident from the conventional sources. Thus, his love letters to his wife are couched in fulsome and cloying English, with only a hint of native idiom and an occasional Gaelic endearment. His formidable and immemorially Gaelic grandmother, Máire Ní Dhuibh, must have deeply impressed him as she did all the family yet one would hardly gather this from the genteel politeness of his enquiry from London:

> I was very sorry to hear of the declining state of my grandmother's health. Assure her of my warmest and sincerest affection and that I shall never forget her tenderness for us all.[26]

His early schooling, before his departure for the Continent, may have included instruction in reading and writing Irish: certainly, that would be the inference from the quite incredible assertion attributed to Tomás Ó Dunlaing, an inspector for the Irish Society, who referred to O'Connell as "the best Irish scholar he had ever met with".[27] However, it is far more likely that O'Connell's acquaintance with Irish was exclusively an instinctive, familiar one which survived the formal educational process.

There was more, of course, to the Gaelic heritage than the language. As Gerard Murphy observes:

> All round him in his boyhood were to be found, almost in full strength, that wealth of peasant poetry, song and folktale, and that Gaelic eloquence and ease of intercourse which, even in a weakened form, have so charmed modern scholars.[28]

At the time of the Ossianic controversy, the young O'Connell recalled that "the names of Ossian's heroes were familiar to my infancy, and long before I had heard of Macpherson or his translation the characters of the poem were mostly known to me".[29] And as well as the *fiannaíocht*,* there was the more mundane tradition of the singers and balladeers at fairs and markets. Late in life, Daunt tells us, "O'Connell would suddenly break out with a snatch of some old ballad in Irish or English" which he had heard long ago on boyhood visits to Tralee.[30] He told the Catholic Association in 1826: "In my own family, there were very good Irish scholars and Irish poets too. Their poetry was indeed pathetic and mournful, for they had reason to be melancholy".[31] According to the *Milesian Magazine*, February 1816, "the great Catholic Demosthenes in his ... impeachment ... of the duke of Richmond lamented that he was restricted in his eloquence by the ignorance of his auditory" of the Irish language.[32] This refers to O'Connell's speech in the Magee trial, in the course of which, according to this magazine, he described the English language as "the pedlar tongue".

There seem to have been times when only Irish could convey his feelings or have the desired effect on his audience, though the public occasions on which he used the language were few. When he addressed a big election meeting at Tralee on New Year's Day, 1835, he moved his audience to tears when he dwelt emotionally, in Irish, on the Rathcormac massacre, the most tragic episode of the tithe war, which had occurred a fortnight previously.[33] According to his contemporary biographer, William Fagan, "it was said to have been the most eloquent speech he ever delivered".[34] He told Daunt that he had made a speech in Irish in 1828 in Co. Louth (then extensively Irish-speaking) and that

---

* Heroic cycle about the Fianna, a legendary war-band in early Ireland.

at Tralee "the reporters from a London journal were ludicrously puzzled at an harangue he delivered in the ancient tongue of Erin".[35]

Contemporary newspapers note various political speeches in Irish at the period.[36] Dominic Phil Ronayne spoke in Irish to repealers in Youghal Catholic Chapel in 1835,[37] as did Fr. J. A. O'Sullivan in Enniskeane in 1842.[38] The noted Cork priest, Fr. Matt Horgan, prayed for O'Connell during grace in Irish at a Skibbereen Repeal dinner in 1843[39] and composed an Irish prayer on the occasion of his imprisonment in 1844.[40] At a great Repeal procession and meeting in Cork city in June 1845, banners bearing Irish slogans were carried, O'Connell's triumphal car was greeted by a historical tableau, and a harper read from a parchment scroll a lengthy and ornate address in Irish to the Liberator: it contained the significant phrase *Ó Conaill na céad cath neamhfhuillteach**.[41] Amhlaoibh Ó Súilleabháin, the diarist, gave an Irish speech at a famous reform and anti-tithe meeting at Ballyhale, Co. Kilkenny in 1832.[42] The Rev. Robert King spoke at length in Irish at a meeting in Co. Louth in the Repeal year of 1843; O'Connell was almost certainly present and, if so, in all probability spoke in Irish too.[43]

If Irish was a political language to an extent not always appreciated by historians, neither was it entirely absent from O'Connell's legal life. A schoolfellow of O'Connell's son, John, tells us that the Liberator arbitrated on local disputes in Derrynane: "Mr. O'Connell... distributed justice all round, and each one seemed to go away well satisfied with the cheap law afforded them by the great impartial lawgiver... All this was in the Irish language, for on average not three of the forty ['peasants'] present could deliver his thoughts in any other tongue".[44] In the law courts, O'Connell's familiarity with Irish words and idiom was an invaluable part of his remarkable powers of cross-examination. This is illustrated in two well-known stories, too lengthy to be retailed here, in which he exposes the deviousness of witnesses.[45] Moreover, it is arguable that much of his mental agility and resourcefulness both as politician and lawyer came from his bilingualism—*an dá arm aigne* in an tAthair Peadar's celebrated phrase,[46] which may be translated as "the two weapons of the mind". All this apart, his knowledge of Irish provided a kind of runic communion between him and the ordinary people and this is illustrated in the folklore.[47]

---

* O'Connell of the hundred non-bloody battles. ("Conn of the hundred battles" was the name of an early Irish king, familiar in the nationalist folklore.)

Can we really speak at all of O'Connell having *attitudes* towards the Irish language? He lived instinctively through Irish at one level of his being, as did the Jacobite MacCarthys a century earlier, and he was not in any case given to analytical reflection on language and culture. The only statement he is alleged to have made on the subject is that recorded in O'Neill Daunt's *Personal Recollections of Daniel O'Connell.* Daunt was present at a private party on St. Patrick's Day 1833 when someone asked the Liberator "whether the use of the Irish language was diminishing among our peasantry". The reply has been so often quoted against O'Connell that I want to reproduce it here in full, though it is worth remembering that these may not be the *ipsissima verba* at all:

> Yes, and I am sufficiently utilitarian not to regret its gradual abandonment. A diversity of tongues is no benefit; it was first imposed on mankind as a curse, at the building of Babel. It would be of vast advantage to mankind if all the inhabitants of the earth spoke the same language. Therefore, although the Irish language is connected with many recollections that twine around the hearts of Irishmen, yet the superior utility of the English tongue, as the medium of all modern communication, is so great, that I can witness without a sigh the gradual disuse of the Irish.[48]

Note that O'Connell uses the word "gradual". There was no way he could have foreseen the rapid post-Famine decline of the language. Again, his nostalgic affection for the ancestral tongue is evident but so, too, is what was to become a common and understandable nineteenth-century view—that English was the norm. When O'Connell spoke about the "superior utility" of the English language, he was simply stating a fact. Not even the most enthusiastic antiquarian advocates of Irish at that period could have denied the limitations of the language as a modern medium—its lack of standardisation, for example. (For that matter, neither could they have foreseen its astonishing adaptability to twentieth-century concepts and terminology). O'Connell's attitude was simply the recognition of a centuries-old linguistic process in Ireland.

His reference to his being "utilitarian" has been commonly taken to mean his application of the principles of Benthamite utilitarianism to the situation. But it is doubtful if political philosophy basically influenced O'Connell on the matter though it would have provided a

convenient rationalisation and, certainly, his enlightenment world-
view made him see things in rational and universal terms. (In this connection, to blame O'Connell for not having identified nationality with
language is somewhat of an anachronism). Essentially, however, his
"utilitarianism" was no more than the pragmatism of the Gaeltacht
man, the working out of those rules of elemental survival which, in
another context, made ready changes of religious allegiance common
enough in the Gaeltacht. Cardinal Tomás Ó Fiaich has drawn our
attention to the contrast of "O'Connell and ... Davis towards Irish—
O'Connell, of Gaelic and Catholic stock, with a fluent knowledge of
the language, seeking to promote English, and Davis, of Anglo–Irish
and Protestant stock, with only a smattering of the language ... calling
for the spread of Irish".[49] It has been ever thus. Until Gaelic League
days at least, few native speakers were language enthusiasts. Even An
tAthair Peadar cast a cold eye on the enthusiasms of the urban Gaelic
Leaguers. Irish won't sell the cow, went the sceptical saying, and
O'Connell would have readily sympathised with the man in Rosmuc
schoolhouse who interrupted Pearse's appeal to cherish the language
by shouting: "*Is beag an mhaith í nuair a ghabhann tú thar an Teach
Dóite*".*[50] "Betterment" is one powerful explanation of voluntary
anglicization in the nineteenth century, and O'Connell exhibited this
characteristic *par excellence*, both in his own person and for the people
he led.

On the question of Irish, O'Connell manifested not only the utilitarianism of the Gaeltacht man but his own individual pragmatic tem-
perament, that of the legal and political animal he essentially was. It is
significant that despite all the self-intoxication of his forensic eloquence, for him the verdict was the thing, as he once asserted.[51] His
view of education, too, was functional—witness his instructions to the
rector of Clongowes for the education of his sons.[52] In his own youthful
study:

> I relax my mind with the study of History and the Belles Lettres,
> objects absolutely necessary for every person who has occasion to
> speak in public, as they enlarge the ideas, and afford that strength
> and solidity of speech which are requisite for every public speaker.[53]

and again:

> While I apply myself to the English language, I endeavour to unite
> purity of diction to the harmony and arrangement of phraseology.[54]

---

* Little good is it when you go beyond the Teach Dóite.

(Indeed, when he wasn't speaking Irish or Hiberno–English, which also had its uses, he used English with all the extravagant eloquence of the educated native Irish speaker! Haven't we all known many such?)

Temperamentally, O'Connell had little sympathy with the antiquarian concern for Irish which characterised scholars in pre-Gaelic League days. According to Eugene O'Curry, the Counsellor was once shown the Irish–English dictionary of the Clare scholar Peter O'Connell whose nephew, Anthony, brought the manuscript to the Tralee assizes "expecting that O'Connell would call public attention to it" but he "had no taste for matters of this kind, and he suddenly dismissed his namesake, telling him that his uncle was an old fool to have spent so much of his life on so useless a work".[55] Equally in character was his contempt for the Annals of the Four Masters:

> They are little more than a bare record of faction or clan fights. 'On such a day the chief of such a place burned the castle of the chief of so-and-so'; there's a tiresome sameness of this sort of uninteresting narrative.[56]

He had a pride, of course, in the aristocratic Gaelic past and relished telling the splendid story of the MacCarthy lady in Paris who refused to lift her head from her embroidery to watch Louis XIV's triumphal entry into the city: she had seen MacCarthy entering Blarney, "and what can Paris furnish to excel that?"[57] In this sense, O'Connell was certainly not devoid of *mórtas cine**.[58] But the *political* concepts in the Gaelic tradition, such as they were, the *aisling*† fantasies of an overseas deliverer restoring a long dead order, were meaningless to his modern mind: for his political nourishment he went to Anglo–Ireland and the wider world beyond.

In his admirable pioneering essay Gerard Murphy suggested that O'Connell abandoned the Gaelic way of life because it was immature, barbaric and at the same time in decay.[59] I do not believe that this kind of decision or choice entered into the matter at all. In any case, early nineteenth century Gaelicism had much more maturity and vitality than Murphy concedes. Nor do I think it true that Irish for O'Connell was simply a *patois*, what Pennsylvania Dutch is today for Americans in that area. His patronage of Tomás Ruadh Ó Súilleabháin indicates a higher level of interest.[60] But Irish was part of O'Connell's life, not of

---

* Pride of race.
† Vision-poetry.

his philosophy. He was bewildered more than antagonised by the manifestations of Young Ireland cultural nationalism. Though bilingual himself, he could not endorse Davis's advocacy of "one language as a medium of commerce, and another as a vehicle of history, the wings of song, ... and a mask and guard of ... nationality",[61] or even Archbishop MacHale's "Keep the Irish which is your own, and learn English".[62]

O'Connell turned a deaf ear to the few enthusiasts who asked him directly to use his influence to have the language cherished. A speaker at a Repeal meeting in Co. Louth appealed to the new Moses, "an t-Ath-Mhaoise" to help re-establish the supremacy of Irish as a step towards freedom (*beidh teanga mhín, mhilis ár máthara air buil againn arís, agus a chur air bonn mar is cóir**).[63] If, as seems almost certain, O'Connell was present on that platform, he could hardly have been pleased by the note of agrarian millenialism in the same speech![64] On another occasion, O'Connell was the recipient of a letter from Rev. Simon Walsh who worked in a Catholic mission in London's East End. Walsh was urging the need for a Catholic bible in Irish to combat the activities of the Bible societies in Ireland. Irish, said Walsh, was "remarkable for its copiousness, strength and poetical elegance. I need not say much to you in its praise for its critical knowledge is, I understand, hereditary in your family. Ireland is indebted to your grand-uncle, Dr. J. O'Connell, for one of the finest and most pathetic historical poems that has [sic] been written in any language". In the course of this letter, Walsh pointedly says that he is glad the Liberator's name has an O in it![65]

The proselytising activities of the Irish Society—a burning question in the 1820s—drew some further comments from O'Connell on the Irish language. The Irish Society's plan to publish an Irish translation of the Scriptures caused the Liberator to make the following remarks at a meeting of the Catholic Association:

> There is not a single individual in Ireland that has ever learned to read Irish only through the medium of the English language. In the entire county of Kerry there are not five persons who can read Irish. In the great county of Cork I will venture to affirm that there are not ten, and in the whole province of Munster, not thirty individuals able to read Irish. And, exclusive of the Catholic clergy, there are not probably one hundred laymen in Ireland capable of reading Irish.[66]

---

* We will have our smooth, sweet maternal tongue in good condition, and established, as is fitting.

And at a later meeting:

> Why, there is not a human being in Kerry that can read Irish who has not first learned to read English ... I again say that there are not two men in Kerry who can read Irish, and do not understand English ... I have been told by my father that he remembered a man who learned to read Irish through the medium of the Latin language. This was the only man he ever heard of, that could read Irish, and did not understand English...[67].

Now, the point is not whether O'Connell was right in his assertions (there is some evidence to the contrary)[68] but rather that he was convinced Irish was almost entirely an oral language. In 1824 he was offered an Irish translation of an anti-Whiteboy address but "did not know if it would be prudent to have it printed, as it would be expensive, and there were very few who could read the Irish language".[69] His beliefs in this regard would not have disposed him to take Irish seriously. Moreover, its association with proselytism was one of several factors which brought the language into disrepute among its nineteenth-century speakers.

We might sum up by suggesting that while O'Connell accepted the extension of English as inevitable and desirable, his attitude was different from that which shamefacedly rejected the Irish language as the badge of inferiority and backwardness. Presumably there were then, as there are to-day, many middle positions between enthusiasm and hostility, between acceptance and rejection.

If we have dwelt at some length on O'Connell's attitude to the Gaelic world, what can we say of that world's attitude to him? There were lone voices, like that of Donnchadh Ó Floinn in 1826, who might blame O'Connell that Irishmen were *in easba léinn a sinsir**.[70] But even those like Fr Simon Walsh,[71] an tAthair Liam MacGearailt of Co. Limerick[72] and Rev. Robert King,[73] who would have wished him to espouse the language, remained nonetheless his fervent admirers. And there is little hint of criticism on this score from contemporary Irish poets, those twilight heirs of the Gaelic tradition. If O'Connell's popularity with his followers waned at times during his career, or if he was *never* popular with certain sections, this was for a variety of reasons, none of them connected with any substantial body of feeling

---

* Lacking the learning of their ancestors.

that he was somehow betraying the Gaelic tradition.[74] Anonymous[75] or otherwise, O'Connell's legions of poetic admirers saw nothing incongruous in hailing him as the destroyer of *búir an Bhéarla, bodaigh an Bhéarla,**[76] the man who would ensure *an bhua age Gaelaibh dá fháil ar lucht Béarla.*†[77] He was saluted by Aodh Mac Domhnaill as *an bile gan táir a d'fhás ón nGaeltacht.*‡[78] His use of English, far from being condemned, was seen as a powerful weapon in a hero's linguistic armoury:

> *Ta Laidin is Gréigis agus Gaeilge 'na bheol*
> *is tuile Shacsbéarla ag teacht chuige 'na cheol*
> *is gach teanga eile léannta chun labhairt le Seon.*§[79]

The encomia pour out from Raifteirí, Diarmuid na Bolgaighe, Seághan Ó Braonáin, Micheál Óg Ó Longáin, Aodh Mac Domhnaill and Diarmuid Ua Mathghamhna.[80] Micheál Mac Cárthaigh silenced those carping critics who would dare ask:

> *créad do rin Connell do mhaitheas riamh dúinn-ne*
> *acht amháin ar bhailigh sé d'airgead púint leis?* ‖[81]

O'Connell is the new Moses, the Phoenix, the Gaelic prince, *ár gCormac Stíobhairt.*¶[82] And whether his novel strategy of constitutional agitation is half-understood and praised—as it sometimes is[83]— or whether he is made to fit in with the old *aisling*** tradition[84] or, even more incongruously, saluted as a physical force man and a precursor of social revolution,[85] he is always the champion, the defender *ag cimeád cúil dúinn.*††[86]

The verses of his protégé, or "court poet", Tomás Ruadh Ó Súilleabháin, are of particular interest in all this.[87] Tomás Ruadh wrote a number of poems in praise of O'Connell, lines of hope, welcome, good wishes—and triumph. Nowhere else do we get the millenial expectations of O'Connell's own people so graphically expressed. And, allowing for literary convention, the expectations were really there. In one

---

* English-speaking boors, English-speaking churls.
† That the Gaels would be victorious over the English-speaking crowd.
‡ A distinguished tree without reproach that grew from the Irish-speaking area.
§ He has Latin and Greek and Irish on his lips, and additionally English coming to him musically. And every other learned language to enable him to converse with John [Bull].
‖ What good did Connell ever do for us, only the pounds of money he gathered for himself?
¶ Our Charles Stuart.
** Vision-poetry.
†† Keeping goal for us.

sense, the Gaelic poets and O'Connell were speaking the same language, metaphorically, that is. "The language of politics for him, as for them," Gearóid Ó Tuathaigh observes, "was apocalyptic, hyperbolic and rhetorical. They were both inheritors, if only in part, of the same tradition".[88] Yet, in another way, their response was quite different from what he wished to convey. For Tomás Ruadh and the others, Catholics would displace Protestants (*beidh an dlí fúinn arís ar theacht Emancipation**).[89] In this simple interpretation of Catholic Emancipation, the exponents of the Gaelic tradition would have been in accord with attorney-general William Saurin, a diehard opponent of Catholic equality.[90] O'Connell's genuine disclaimers of aiming at Catholic supremacy and his new-fangled ideas of real religious equality were totally eclipsed in the sectarian tumult of the times: they were simply ignored by those who saw him as their champion against *slíocht Luther an éithigh is Calvin chaim chraosaigh*†.[91] The most celebrated verse of Tomás Ruadh best expresses what the whole O'Connell phenomenon meant to the Gaelic world. It was part of a poem composed for the great welcome home after the Clare election:

> *Sé Domhnall binn Ó Conaill caoin*
> *An planda fíor den Ghaedheal-fhuil*
> *Gur le foghluim dlí is meabhair a chinn*
> *Do scól sé síos an craes-shliocht*
> *Go bhfuil sé scríofa i bPastorina*
> *Go maithfear cíos do Ghaelaibh*
> *'S go mbeidh farraigí breac le flít ag teacht*
> *Isteach thar pointe Chléire.*‡[92]

O'Connell's Gaelic background, then, is central to a full appreciation of the man and his relations with the people. As Seán de Fréine suggests, had he been born a generation later and subjected to different influences, instead of being a national leader he might well have been "the first Irish Catholic to be Lord Chief Justice of England."[93] As it was, he was close to the end of the Gaelic tradition in his family. Admittedly, his eldest son Maurice spoke Irish. When he was nearly

---

* The law will be under ourselves [under our direction] again when Emancipation comes.
† The descendants of lying Luther and crooked avaricious Calvin.
‡ It is sweet and gentle Daniel O'Connell who is the true plant of Gaelic blood, Who with legal learning and mental sharpness, Did beat down the greedy brood, And it is written in Pastorina, That rent will be remitted to Gaels. And the seas will be speckled with fleets coming In by the headland of Cleire.

two years old, Mary O'Connell reported: "He talks a great deal but all in Irish".[94] In 1845 the journalist William Howard Russell observed: "And there was Maurice O'Connell [at Derrynane]... talking Irish to the boys and colleens, who laughed at his jokes as if they were at a fair or a wedding".[95] However, Maurice was hardly typical; and we must still see the truth in H. G. Dutton's words in his *Survey of Galway* in 1824: "In the next generation, there will not probably be a gentleman that will be able to speak Irish."[96]

Later generations which saw the rapid decline of the Irish language and its distinctive culture as calamitous looked for convenient anglicising agents and readily found them in Maynooth, the National Schools and Daniel O'Connell, the latter being the chief scapegoat. Whether his attitudes made much difference to the fortunes of a virtually doomed language, in view of what we now know of the complex phenomena of linguistic change, is very doubtful. But what is certain is that for his own people he was the last hero of the Gaelic world.[97]

Notes

1. Gerard Murphy, "The Gaelic Background", M. Tierney (ed.), *Daniel O'Connell* (Dublin, 1949), pp. 1–24.
2. For the background to what follows here, see the essays in Brian Ó Cuiv (ed.), *A View of the Irish Language* (Dublin, 1969), particularly Maureen Wall, "The Decline of the Irish Language"; Tomás Ó Fiaich, "The Language and Political History"; and the maps (with note) on pp. 137–40.
3. Mrs. M. J. O'Connell, *The Last Colonel of the Irish Brigade: Count O'Connell and Old Irish Life at home and abroad, 1745–1833* (London, 1892), ii, 253 refers to an occasion when Daniel O'Connell and his uncle, General Daniel O'Connell, conversed in French and fell back on Irish only when somebody who knew French entered the room.
4. (London, 1825), p. 745. See also Tomás de Bhaldraithe's introduction (pp. xxii–xxiv) to his edition of *Cín Lae Amhlaoibh* (Dublin, 1970).
5. Rev. S. Walsh to Daniel O'Connell, 23 October 1824, Maurice R. O'Connell (ed.), *The Correspondence of Daniel O'Connell*, (Ireland, 1972–1980), III, Letter 1136, argues against the proposition that "few people can read the Irish language". But the evidence of Tomás Ó Dunlaing (who was an inspector for The Irish Society for the Promotion of the Education of the Native Irish through the Medium of their Own Language) supports the proposition: see T. F. O'Rahilly, "Tomás Ó Dunlaing agus Seán Ó Braonáin", *Celtica*, i (1950), 309–310.
6. See map in Ó Cuiv (ed.), *A view of the Irish Language*, p. 138.

7. William J. O'N. Daunt, *Personal Recollections of the late Daniel O'Connell*, M.P. (London, 1848), i, 36-7.
8. *O'Connell Correspondence*, i, 276 (references throughout are to *letter* numbers).
9. Daunt, *Recollections*, i, 164-66.
10. *O'Connell Correspondence*, i, 305.
11. Ibid., i, 436.
12. Ibid., i, 441.
13. E.g. 1812, 1813, 1814: see ibid., i, 395, 446, 499.
14. Ibid., i, 499.
15. Quoted in R. Moley, *Daniel O'Connell* (New York, 1974), p. 31.
16. *O'Connell Correspondence*, i, 422.
17. Ibid., i, 254.
18. Derrynane remained especially so, at least until the Coomakishta road opened up access in 1839.
19. 2 vols (London, 1892): see n. 3.
20. Cf. Daunt, *Recollections*, i, 155.
21. Hewitt's Journal for 1846, cited in Ó Súilleabháin, *Beatha* (see note 25 below), p. 201; also see *ibid.*, pp. 240-1.
22. E.g., in 1814 we find him drawing up marriage articles ("they will give me the delay of a day or two") for his first cousin, Con O'Leary: *O'Connell Correspondence*, i, 473. O'Leary was the eldest child of Art Ó Laoghaire and Eibhlín Dubh, and is mentioned in the *Caoineadh*—"Conchubhar beag an cheana": see Seán Ó Tuama (ed.), *Caoineadh Airt Uí Laoghaire* (Dublin, 1961), pp. 12, 34.
23. *Irish Historical Studies*, xvii, no. 66 (September 1970), pp. 200-20.
24. D. Corkery, *The Fortunes of the Irish Language* (Dublin, 1954), pp. 112-14. Cf. D. P. Moran, *The Philosophy of Irish Ireland*, 2nd ed., (Dublin, 1905), p. 43: "He did more than any other man, because he was a giant, to kill the Gaelic Language and the distinctive character of the people".
25. J. J. O'Kelly (Sceilg), *O'Connell Calling* (Tralee, 1947), pp. 231-33; A. Ó Duibhir, *Domhnal Ó Conaill* (Dublin, 1949), pp. 349-50; D. Ó Súilleabháin, *Beatha Dhomhnaill Uí Chonaill* (Dublin, 1936), pp. 124-26. Also see P. S. O'Hegarty, *A History of Ireland under the Union* (London, 1952), p. 613.
26. *O'Connell Correspondence*, i, 10. He sends her his regards in other letters: ibid., i, 2, 8, 9.
27. O'Rahilly, "Tomás Ó Dunlaing etc", *Celtica*, i, (1950), 309-10.
28. Murphy, in Tierney (ed.), *Daniel O'Connell*, p. 3.
29. In his journal, 7 December 1796: quoted in Murphy, *loc. cit.*
30. Daunt, *Recollections*, i, 135.
31. Speech of O'Connell at meeting of New Catholic Association, 29 April 1826, reported in *The Dublin Weekly Register* (Supplement), 6 May 1826.
32. *Milesian Magazine*, February 1816, p. 21.
33. See Gerard J. Lyne, "The Kerry Elections of 1835", *Journal of the Kerry Archaeological and Historical Society*, no. 4, (1971), p. 84.

34. Fagan, *The life and times of Daniel O'Connell*, ii (Cork, 1848), 336-7.
35. Daunt, *Recollections*, i, 15.
36. I am indebted to Miss Maura Murphy for the next five references.
37. *Cork Constitution*, 17 February 1835.
38. *Cork Examiner*, 9 December 1842.
39. *Cork Constitution*, 24 June 1843.
40. The prayer is dated 12 August 1844: Horgan MSS, Royal Irish Academy.
41. *Cork Examiner*, 9 June 1845.
42. de Bhaldraithe (ed.), *Cín Lae Amhlaoibh*, p. 101. See also Séamus P. Ó Mórdha's account of "An anti-Tithe speech in Irish", in *Éigse*, vol. i, pt. iv, pp. 223-26.
43. Breandán Ó Buachalla, "A Speech in Irish on Repeal", *Studia Hibernica*, no. 10 (1970), pp. 84-94.
44. Wm. M. N. Skelly, *Diary of a Tour in Munster*, quoted in John J. Horgan, "O'Connell—The Man", Tierney (ed.), *Daniel O'Connell*, p. 289.
45. Cf. Ó Súilleabháin, *Beatha*, pp. 80, 88-89, 125.
46. An tAthair Peadar Ua Laoghaire, *Mo Sgéal Fein* (Dublin, 1915), pp. 35-6.
47. In this connection, the most popular piece of folklore concerns the warning given to O'Connell at a London banquet by a serving-girl not to touch his poisoned drink.
　　One variant goes as follows:

Cailín:　　　*"A Dhomhnaill Uí Chonaill, an dtuigeann tú Gaoluinn?"*
ÓConaill:　*"Tuigim go maith, agus a maireann dem ghaoltaibh".*
Cailín;　　　*"Tá stuif ar do chuid-se ná fuil ar chuid éinne;*
　　　　　　　Ith do dhothain agus ná h-ól aon rud;
　　　　　　　Agus, a Dhomhnaill Uí Chonaill, ná feicim-se tréith thú."
ÓConaill:　*"Is maith thú, a chailín; bhéarfad-sa spré dhuit".*

(cf. Ó Súilleabháin, *Beatha*, p. 262).

Girl:　　　　Daniel O'Connell, do you understand Irish?
O'Connell:　I do well, and so do my surviving relatives.
Girl:　　　　There's stuff in your portion [of drink] that isn't in anybody else's;
　　　　　　　Eat your fill and do not drink anything;
　　　　　　　And, Daniel O'Connell, that I may not see you feeble.
O'Connell:　Good girl! I'll get a dowry for you.

From a folklorist's viewpoint, an interesting feature of the story is its occurrence in widely different parts of the country.
48. Daunt, *Recollections*, i, 14-15. Daunt's own attitude to the language (admittedly, expressed at a much later date) was very different from that of O'Connell. He lamented its rapid decline, strongly deplored the people's "wretched, servile, contemptible indifference" to its preservation, and saw no reason why our people should not, like the Welsh, be bilingual...": William J. O'N. Daunt, *A Life Spent for Ireland* (London, 1896), pp. 385 (29 August 1883), 391 (23 July 1884).

49. Ó Fiaich, in Ó Cuiv (ed.), *A View of the Irish Language*, p. 109.
50. Maureen Wall, ibid., p. 87. The Teach Dóite was regarded as a cultural frontier with the English-speaking world outside.
51. Quoted by Horgan, in Tierney (ed.), *Daniel O'Connell*, p. 300.
52. *O'Connell Correspondence*, ii, 508.
53. Ibid., i, 12.
54. Ibid., i, 20.
55. See Murphy, in Tierney (ed.), *Daniel O'Connell*, p. 5 and n.
56. Daunt, *Recollections*, i, 47. Was O'Connell simply repeating somebody else's opinion? In any case, no satisfactory edition/translation was available during his lifetime: see John O'Donovan's intro., *Annals of the Kingdom of Ireland by the Four Masters* (Dublin, 1856), vol. i.
57. Daunt, *Recollections*, i, 45.
58. There is plenty of evidence that O'Connell took pride in his family lineage though he was not preoccupied with the subject. Also it is of interest to note that during the peace resolutions debate on 13 July 1846 he referred to O'Conor Don as "the highest name in the country": *Nation*, 18 July 1846.
59. See Murphy's essay generally but especially pp. 5–6, 20, 22–24, in Tierney (ed.), *Daniel O'Connell*.
60. See below p. 27.
61. Quoted by Ó Fiaich, in Ó Cuiv (ed.), *A View of the Irish Language*, p. 110.
62. Quoted by Wall, ibid., p. 86.
63. *Studia Hibernica*, (1970), p. 93.
64. Ibid.
65. This is the letter mentioned in n. 5 above. I am indebted to Professor Maurice O'Connell for drawing this, and other items, to my attention. The poem referred to would seem to be "Tuireamh na hÉireann" (c. 1650) by Seán Ó Conaill: see *Five Seventeenth-Century Political Poems* edited by Cecile O'Rahilly (Dublin 1952), pp. 50–82. But the author could hardly have been the Liberator's grand-uncle!
66. *The Morning Register*, 24 April 1825, p. 4. Professor Pádraig de Brún drew this and the following extract to my attention.
67. *The Dublin Weekly Register*, 6 May 1826.
68. See the Walsh letter mentioned in n. 5.
69. Cf. Pádraig de Brún, "Forógra do Ghaelaibh 1824", *Studia Hibernica*, no. 12 (1972), pp. 142ff.
70. I must thank Professor Breandán Ó Buachalla, University College, Dublin, for this and a number of references to verses on O'Connell. Professor Seán Ó Coileáin of University College, Cork, also helped with identifying the sources of various Gaelic verses.
71. See the Walsh letter mentioned in n. 5 and n. 65.
72. He was long remembered for his excellent sermons in Irish, and spoke in Irish at a meeting in 1825 in Newcastle West, to promote the Catholic Rent: see de Brún in *Studia Hibernica* (1972), pp. 142ff.
73. See n. 43 and n. 63 above.
74. Nioclás Ó Cearnaigh, in verses of satirical comment on the peace resolu-

tion debates in 1846, sharply criticised the policy of rejecting physical force under all circumstances: Royal Irish Academy 23 E 12, p. 271.

75. I am indebted to Dr Maura Murphy for showing me copies of street ballads on O'Connell, preserved among the Outrage Papers in Dublin Castle and in the Bradshaw Irish Collection in Cambridge. See, for example, "The Humours of Innishannon", a ballad sheet printed entirely in phonetic Irish, sung in Kinsale, January 1833 (Chief Secretary's Office, Registered Papers: Outrage Reports, 1833/1); "Orange Grief or Colleen Beg na Luachra", sung in Dunmanway, April 1841, with alternating English and Irish stanzas (CSORP: OR 6. 13273); and "Eastig a Deena", with similarly alternating verses (Bradshaw Irish Collection, v, 307).

76. Cliches in Irish poetry since the seventeenth century: in the present context, see another ballad on O'Connell, "An Irish Elegy", (c. 1835), by James O'Brien, in Bradshaw Irish Collection, v, 392.

77. Aodh Mac Domhnaill of Co. Meath, unpublished verses: Professor Ó Buachalla has supplied this and the next two references.

78. Aodh Mac Domhnaill, see n. 77.

79. Anon (Prof. Ó Buachalla's reference).

80. Diarmuid na Bolgaighe's "Domhnall Ó Conaill" is in Seán Ó Súilleabháin (ed.), *Diarmuid na Bolgaighe agus a chomhursain* (Dublin, 1937), pp. 45–47. Pádraig de Brún (ed.), *Filíocht Sheáin Uí Bhraonáin* (Dublin, 1972), poem no. 25 and index sub Ó Conaill, Domhnall. See Micheál Óg Ó Longáin, "Gura fada buan bhéas Domhnall", RIA, 23 C 8, p. 403. For more poetic tributes to O'Connell, see Gearóid Ó Tuathaigh, "The Folk-Hero and Tradition", *The World of Daniel O'Connell*, (ed.) Donal McCartney (Dublin and Cork, 1980), pp. 34ff.

81. See his "Duain ar bhás Dhomhnaill Uí Chonaill", in Eoin Ua Riain (ed.), *Féilsgríbhinn Eoin Mhic Néill* (Dublin, 1940), pp. 93–96. The "duain" is presented by Torna, and the line here quoted is on p. 95.

82. Of these and other descriptions, the most interesting is *an t-Ath-Mhaoise*, the "new" or "second Moses", which is a recurring theme: see Ó Buachalla, in *Studia Hibernica* (1970), p. 93 and Tomás Ruadh Ó Súilleabháin's poem, "Cuimhnigidh mar tháinig Maois" in *Amhráin Thomáis Ruaidh*, ed. "Séamus Dubh" (Dublin, 1914), p. 58. Aodh Mac Domhnaill depicts him as "Maoise ag sárú Éigipt" (Moses overcoming Egypt), *Dhá Chéad de Cheoltaibh Uladh*, ed. Enrí Ó Muirgheasa (Dublin, 1969), p. 38.

83. By, for example, Eoghan Ó Comhraidhe and Aodh Mac Domhnaill. The latter says:

> *Ní le gunnaí nó púdar a thug sé an chliú leis*
> *ó Bhreatanaigh bhrúidiúil is a bpáirtí*
> *acht le briathra breá cumhra mar bholadh na n-úlla.*

> Not with guns or powder did he take away fame with him.
> From the brutish Britons and their followers
> But· with fine fragrant words like the scent of apples.

(Colm Beckett, "Dónal Dílis Ó Chontae Chiarraí", *An tUltach*, Nollaig 1975, p. 5). See Eoghan Ó Comhraidhe's poem celebrating the Clare election victory, "A eigse Chinn Choradh", *Irisleabhar na Gaedhilge*, Vol. VIII, No. 88 (Aug. 1897), pp. 69–70.

Micheál MacCárthaigh (see n. 81) asks rhetorically:

cia bhuaigh ar ghallaibh na Breataine an báire.
gan gunna, gan claidheamh, gan saighead chum sáidhte,
gan fiú fuil chreabhair do leith foghla ar a ghárda?

Who won the game against the foreigners of Britain,
Without a gun, without a sword, without an arrow for sticking
And without suffering the loss of his own side of even so much as a
woodcock's blood?

84. As in Diarmuid Ua Mathghamhna's *aisling*, *Gadelica*, i, 16–18.
85. As in the last stanza of Ua Mathghamhna's *aisling*; also see "Orange Grief", referred to in n. 74. Rev. Robert King in his speech in Irish in Co. Louth (see n. 43 and n. 63) ties in Repeal with language revival and the social millenium. See also Tomás Ruadh's stanza quoted on p. 28 below.
86. Diarmuid Ua Mathghamhna, in *Gadelica*, i, 16–18. "Ní baolach dúinn choíche", says Raifteirí, "chomh fad is mhairfeas Ó Conaill" (We'll never be in any danger as long as O'Connell lives). Dubhglas de hide (ed.), *Abhráin agus Dánta an Reachtabhraigh* (Dublin 1969), p. 61.
87. *Amhráin Thomáis Ruaidh* (ed. "Séamus Dubh"), Dublin, 1914. In a letter dated 27 June 1825 to O'Connell's land agent, John Primrose, Jr., Mary O'Connell says: "I believe the Poet who has been here this some time is gone back in the same vessel with the furniture [consigned by sea to Derrynane]. I suppose he will return to his own place, and set up a school if he can succeed in getting scholars. I am sure he will be an acquisition in that country." (MSS 13, 645, National Library of Ireland). Mary could not speak Irish so that she could only have judged Tomás Ruadh as an English-speaking man.

Among the Fitz-Simon Papers (property of Lt.-Col M. O'Connell Fitz-Simon, M. C., Glencullen House, Kiltiernan, Co. Dublin) there are two English poems of poor quality by Tomás Ruadh, one lauding O'Connell's "white house in Merrion Square" and the other in praise of a niece of Mary O'Connell's who is about to be married. I am obliged to Professor Maurice O'Connell for drawing this information to my attention.

88. See Gearóid Ó Tuathaigh, "Gaelic Ireland, Popular Politics and Daniel O'Connell", *Journal of the Galway Archaeological and Historical Society*, 1975, pp. 21–34.
89. *Amhráin Thomáis Ruaidh*, p. 96.
90. Cf. R. B. McDowell, *Public Opinion and Government Policy in Ireland, 1801–46* (London, 1952), pp. 86–7.
91. "Cuimhnigidh mar tháinig Maois", *Amhráin Thomáis Ruaidh*, p. 58.
92. "Sé Domhnall Binn Ó Conaill Caoin", *Amhráin Thomáis Ruaidh*, 58.
93. S. de Fréine, *The Great Silence* (Dublin, 1965), p. 170.

94. *O'Connell Correspondence*, i, 144.
95. John B. Atkins, *Life of Sir William Howard Russell*, (London, 1911), I, p. 33.
96. Quoted in O'Hegarty, *Ireland under the Union*, p. 395.
97. See Ó Tuathaigh, "The Folk-Hero and Tradition," *The World of Daniel O'Connell*, (ed.) McCartney.

4

O'Connell in Irish Folk Tradition

Diarmaid Ó Muirithe

Johann Georg Köhl, a German librarian who visited Ireland a few years before O'Connell's death, considered that he had had the privilege of witnessing a rare and somewhat mysterious occurrence, the emergence of a new national folk-hero. The extraordinary thing was that the person being elevated to the status of hero was still alive, a phenomenon the German scholar tried to explain as follows:

> The Irish are a people after the old model, a people almost without a counterpart in the world. In Germany, we have everywhere become too enlightened and too self-dependent for any authority. We laugh at all who call themselves prophets; but among the Irish the old faith in saints and miracles still exists. Here alone, the mighty, the immortal and the great still find a fertile soil whence to obtain laurels and a halo. Add to this that O'Connell is an extraordinary man, a man of power, authority and wealth by means and ways hitherto unheard of in this world; and who, without employing any physical force, and without making any concessions, has, for 40 years, raised an opposition against the most powerful aristocracy in Europe, while, on his part, he has had almost nothing but a few millions of beggars as supporters.[1]

O'Connell himself must have heard in his youth the various types of stories that grew around people acknowledged to be especially gifted—poets, for example—and no doubt he understood the process that made himself one of the laochra—the heroes. As one of that elite he was a product of the people's imagination, but, as has been said, imagination is not the faculty of making something out of nothing, but of using, in more or less different form, something already present in the mind. O'Connell was given the characteristics of folk heroes of long ago; he was not deified, it is true, as Fionn was, and Cuchulainn, but some of the elements involved in the transmutation of a human into a superhuman are there nonetheless.

First of all, it was to be expected that the new hero's birth and early life should be invested with fantastical qualities. A story from Baile Mhúirne in West Cork claims that at his birth an echo was tossed back and forth between the mountains of Kerry, "so that there wasn't a man or woman who didn't know that some great thing was after happening".[2] The same story used to be told about the birth of another folk-hero, the poet Eoghan Rua Ó Súilleabháin.[3] In this instance O'Connell was made the subject of an older native tale; in other cases he became the hero of well-known international tales. He was, of course, predestined for greatness and the Almighty played His part:

> Dan's father and mother were a good few years married and no sign of a child. They were this day out for a stroll, and the rain came on them and they far from home. They took shelter in a small chapel, a miserable little hut that had a leaky roof of rushes on it. When the rain stopped they went to the parish priest to enquire why he had such a miserable mass-house. "Oh," said the priest, "the parish is too poor to provide better". "We're rich people" said old O'Connell, "and we want for nothing, and we'll give you whatever it will cost to build a new chapel". And they did. The day the first mass was said there, they were, of course, invited, and the priest asked them if there was anything troubling them or if there was anything they wanted. They said that they were childless. When the mass was being said the priest turned to the people and told them to pray now for the couple who had given them their new church, so that they'd have the child they wanted. And nine months after that Daniel O'Connell was born. And when he was born there was a cross on his back, like you'd see on an ass, and that was a sign that he'd be a famous man and that he'd emancipate the Catholics.[4]

A folk-hero should have a distinguished pedigree and according to a West Cork tradition, O'Connell was descended from Diancecht, the great physician of the Tuatha Dé Danann.[5] The first clothes the infant O'Connell wore were, so the storytellers say, passed around from house to house, as they were thought to contain great curative properties;[6] when the infant grew to manhood pieces of his cloaks were in great demand as they were thought to cure a variety of illnessess—just as did the cloaks of the kings of long ago.[7]

A folk-hero is expected to show remarkable talents in his youth, and so it is with the O'Connell of the popular imagination. A story from County Waterford says that a poor farmer once borrowed a horse from a rich neighbour and that the rich man claimed compensation when the horse was accidentally killed: the rich farmer was able to afford the services of the famous Kerry poet Eoghan Rua Ó Súilleabháin as his advocate in deciding the claim, but the poor farmer was, in the words of the storyteller, 'in and out of the room and nobody could he get to help him'. In desperation the poor man called a young boy who was walking to school with a bundle of books under his arm. The storyteller continues:

> He told the boy what his trouble was and the boy went into the room. Eoghan Rua said to him: "Is it you that's going to settle the price of the horse?"
>
> "I am," said the boy.
>
> "I'm in a hurry," said Eoghan Rua, "and I'll have to fix the price of the horse in three words from both sides".
>
> "All right," said the boy.
>
> "I'll have the first three words," said Eoghan Rua—"Trí fichid punt!* I've said my say. Now it's your turn".
>
> "Lá an Bhreithiúntais,"† said the boy, and what he meant was, that the poor man would have that much time to pay. And that boy was Daniel O'Connell. And that was how he got the better of Eoghan Rua.[8]

The important thing to remember about this story is that the child had got the better of an accepted folk-hero, a man of wit and learning and a poet of great distinction. Here, undoubtedly, was a child of promise. This victory foretold greatness as a lawyer, and as such O'Connell is imbued with another of the folk-hero's virtues, a certain malicious inventiveness in the face of overwhelming odds. O'Connell the Counsellor is a greater hero than O'Connell the Politician. Perhaps the people he led did not fully understand the complications of the political process, whereas the legal process they were all too familiar with. At any rate the stories about the great Counsellor are full of an exuberant inventiveness. One example is the story of the man who assaulted a bailiff—a hanging matter in those days. O'Connell agreed to defend him.

> "The only thing you can do," said O'Connell "is to pretend you are dead. Here's money: go and provide yourself with a good wake".

---

* Three score pounds.
† The Judgement Day.

O'Connell happened to have an English visitor in his house at the time and he brought him along to the wake. They had great fun at the wake; the Englishman drank and smoked and played games and made love and even said a prayer for the corpse. When the case was called, O'Connell called him as a witness, and the Englishman swore that there was no use proceeding with the case: he saw the defendant dead; wasn't he himself at his wake? The case was finished there and then. A few days later didn't the bailiff meet the corpse on the road. He took such a fright that he left the country and never came back any more![9]

The story of the Doneraile Conspiracy and of O'Connell's night ride from Derrynane to Cork to defend the men involved is well known. This story has got curiously interwoven with an old Blasket story concerning the crew of a fishing boat brought from Kerry to stand trial for smuggling in Belfast, and as an example of how a folktale grows, the story is interesting:

There was a crew of a boat in Uíbh Ráthach a great many years ago and they were smuggling something in from a vessel and they were caught, of course; and they were taken to Belfast where they were to be sentenced. And it happened that some landlord came into the prison and he saw them and they complained their case to him.

"Musha, poor men," says he, "you're the pity. Is there anyone that could help you? "There is one man," said one of them, "and if he was here, he'd speak for us".

"And where is that man?" said the landlord.

"He's in Derrynane, in Kerry, in Uíbh Ráthach," the man said, "and his name is Daniel O'Connell, and he's a counsellor and he's very good".

"Oh, God be with us," said the landlord, "he's too far away," says he, "but I promise you this much: I'll do my best for you".

He went off then, the landlord, and he didn't stop until he went to a man of his acquaintance who kept racehorses, and he had the best horse in Ireland. He offered him £100 if he'd go to Derrynane and bring Daniel O'Connell. The man took the money and he didn't draw rein until he came to Derrynane and told Daniel O'Connell the story.

"Oh, tut tut!" said Daniel when he heard the story, "I'll be too late. We haven't much time to get there". He dragged out his own horse, and off they went to Belfast. And so fast they went that when they arrived, Daniel's horse fell dead under him. Most of the case was heard by this time and things looked bad for the men from Uíbh Rathach. But Daniel the Counsellor spoke up and he said: "I'm speaking for these men, Judge; don't give your judgement yet". "And who are you?" said the Judge. "I can't put back the clock or reverse the law—my judgment is given," he said.

"Ambasa,"* said Daniel O'Connell, "I'm Daniel O'Connell," he said, "and I'm a counsellor of repute, as knowledgeable as you or any judge in the place, and put your court in action again," he said, "otherwise you'll never again sit in that chair. And it isn't here the case should be heard but back in Derrynane in Uíbh Rathach, where they did whatever they did".

"Ambasa," said the judge, "but you're right. Have it your own way. Take them to Derrynane".

The men were let out and taken to Derrynane, and I suppose Daniel O'Connell wasn't too hard on them. Whatever they were charged with, it wasn't very much. And I heard they were let off.[10]

As a politician and lawyer, O'Connell was, in the minds of the people, the lone Champion fighting their cause in a foreign land where his life was constantly threatened. The story of O'Connell and the Irish servant girl who warned him that a glass of wine put before him at a dinner party was poisoned is well known; indeed a version of the conversation between them has reached the folklore of the Scottish Isles. A Munster version has it:

> A Dhónaill Uí Chonaill, a' dtuigeann tú Gaolainn?
> Tuigim, a chailín, is a mhaireann dem' ghaolta.
> Tá an iomarca salainn sa ghloinne san taobh leat,
> Mas fíor san, a chailín, is maith í do spré-se.†[11]

If one were to believe some of the stories, O'Connell had no need to fear the poisoned cup. Like another hero of old, he was invulnerable, except in the heel![12]

All great champions, of course, must prove themselves in armed combat and Dan's one and only duel wasn't enough for the storytellers. So other adversaries were invented.

One time O'Connell had to fight a duel in London. The greatest swordsman in England was against him. He was no match for Dan.

* A mild expletive.
† 'Daniel O'Connell, do you understand Irish?'
  'I do, girl, and so do all my relations'.
  'There's too much salt in that glass in front of you'.
  'If that's true, girl, you'll get a good dowry'.

Time and time again, the Counsellor got through the Englishman's guard only to find that his sword buckled on the Englishman's chest. The Englishman was wearing a vest of armour, unknown to Dan. He'd be there yet getting nowhere only for that an Irish boy in the crowd, knowing the secret, called out to him: "A Donaill, conas a mharófá muc age baile?" Dan saw what he meant. He lunged at the Englishman's throat and killed him.[13]

Usually O'Connell did not have to rely on help from his friends to outwit the enemy. The phenomenal mental agility usually associated with folk-heroes took care of things. A Sligo storyteller illustrated the point in making O'Connell the hero of an international tale, *The Cat and The Candle*. To make a long story short, an Englishman bet O'Connell that his two cats would hold up two candles all during dinner. O'Connell took two mice from ⹂is pocket, and accordingly won his bet.[14]

Many's the time, the storytellers assure us, O'Connell perplexed the Westminster Parliament with ruses and trickery. According to one storyteller he made quite an impression in his first week as Member for Clare:

When Daniel O'Connell was going forward for election as Member of Parliament (in London), an English member said that if O'Connell sat in the House of Parliament, he would shoot himself. O'Connell was elected, and the first day he sat in the House, he kept his hat firmly on his head. He was ordered to remove it, but he asked to be allowed to keep it on, as he had a bad headache. Permission was granted. Next day, he wore his hat again, as his headache hadn't improved. The third day, he wore his hat again and kept his head bent down, as he still had the headache. On the fourth day he entered the house with his head in the air, and his hat on, and everybody knew that his headache had left him. He was asked how his head was, and he said he felt fine. "Won't you remove your hat, then?" they asked him. "I won't", he replied. "Whatever passes three days in Parliament becomes law". So he kept his hat on, and did so all the time he was a member, although everybody was bareheaded. He kept looking around him, and somebody asked him, "How do you like this House?" "I like it very well", he replied, "but I'm greatly surprised that it doesn't collapse with a perjurer inside it". The man who had sworn to shoot himself heard the remark and he went out into the yard and shot himself.[15]

It is interesting that in the Rosses, County Donegal, an impoverished parish that until very recently depended on the earnings of seasonal labourers in the fields of Scotland, O'Connell the gifted public orator is best remembered. These labourers, potato-pickers and railway navvies, gave O'Connell unswerving loyalty and followed him in their thousands on his triumphant tour of the Scottish cities in 1835. They became known to the native Scots as 'the Dans', and to the present day, the challenge of slum children to one another in the school playgrounds of Glasgow is: 'are you a Billy or a Dan?'.

Nowhere was O'Connell more warmly welcomed than by the Donegal labourers in Scotland. They heard him speak in a hostile environment, they wondered at his courage and at his great gift of oratory, although many of them may not have understood him fully. Their children and grandchildren were told stories about the great man. A woman from Keadue in the Rosses told me, a few months before her 104th birthday, that her mother, who had heard O'Connell speak in Glasgow, insisted that "when O'Connell used to go out in his garden practising a speech, the birds used to stop their singing to listen in admiration".[16] "An fear a chuir draíocht ina luí le fuinneamh a ghlóir", was what the Waterford poet, Pádraig Ó Míleadha, called him, echoing the sentiment.*[17]

A Kerry storyteller asserts that O'Connell's great gift of oratory came to him through his grandmother Máire Ní Dhuibh, a poet:

> The Counsellor and John Sigerson used to oppose one another in law cases and John used to say to him that it wasn't through scholarship that Dan used to best him but through poetry he got through an old hag of a grandmother he had.[18]

In many places people told stories about O'Connell's fabulous virility. Rathkeale in County Limerick, stands indicted as being the only town in Ireland that didn't provide a woman for his bed;[19] his mistresses were legion and they included Queen Victoria.[20]

Even some of the stories concerning O'Connell, the great advocate, have sexual overtones. One story has it that while out on horseback near Derrynane, the Liberator overheard a dispute between some children. The dispute was resolved by a curly-haired boy who argued the case so persuasively that the Counsellor enquired of him who he was. "They say I'm a son of Daniel O'Connell", replied the boy.[21] All these stories are a product of the folk-mind. The heroes of old, on

* The man whose strength of voice made magic.

which the O'Connell of folklore is to a great degree modelled, were ever famous for their sexual energy.[22]

The storytellers did not destroy truth in their making of this new folk-hero, if they embroidered it a little for the sake of their art. Their stories are interesting in a hundred ways not least of which is that they are a mirror of the new democracy their subject had created almost single-handed, a democracy of hope and pride and honour. He had lifted the people from their knees and they, in return, paid him the supreme compliment of making him a hero.

Theirs, of course, was still a very vital folk-art, whereas Gaelic poetry was at the time in a state of decay. Theirs was a truly popular literature, in the best sense, whereas all the poets could do was to sing of the return of princes who had long ceased to exist, or of imminent foreign invasions, in verse that had lost its music and its magic. Reality lent nothing to Gaelic verse in O'Connell's time. Tomás Rua Ó Súilleabháin, a schoolmaster and one of O'Connell's tenants, hoped that another Spanish Armada would come to the aid of his patron, and his idea of a post-Repeal Ireland is typical of the political naïveté of most of the Gaelic poets of the time.

> Agus aisling aréir tríom néall gur deineadh dom
> Go mbeadh Éire againne-ne gan pingin den chíos,
> Agus Sasanaigh an tsaoil seo gan tae gan puins acu,
> Gan piléir ina ngunnaí, gan loingeas ar linn;
> Mar bharr ar a bpéin ní bheidh daonna anois acu,
> Daor is dá bhfeicinn iad in Ifreann thíos
> Agus clanna bochta Gael i ngaorthaíbh cluthara
> Ag bréagadh bruinneall fé dhuilliúr na gcraobh.
> Agus tiocfaidh an Franncach le fogha na maidne ortha
> Cé toghail mar a mheasfaidh siad gan géilleadh dhó,
> Is beidh dlithe na nGall as an mball seo scaipithe
> Beidh teampaill bheannaithe agus cléir gan chol;
> Tiocfaidh an Spáinneach go fíochmhar is a míltí seabhac mear
> Agus réabfaidh glaiseanna do Ghaeil, cé docht,
> Is is mithid dár Stíobhard suí inár mbailte poirt,
> Sin crích agaibh ar Bhanba is is daor é a toisc.*[23]

---

* I saw in a vision while I slept last night
That we'd have Ireland without a penny rent,
And the English of this world without tea or punch,
Without bullets in their guns or ships on the sea;
Worse still, they would have no friends,
Damned, I'd see them in hell below,

The most significant thing about the songs written about O'Connell in Irish was the attitude of the poets to the Counsellor's policy of constitutional agitation. Perhaps it was the influence of the secret agrarian societies, perhaps it was the extension of the mythology that demanded prowess in arms from a champion; in any case, the hero of Derrynane was expected to lead his people into battle. Tomás Ruá Ó Súilleabháin assured his listeners that O'Connell was ready, his blood-sword in his hand:

> Tá an scafaire Dónall, i bhfoirm is i gcóir
> Is claíomh fola ina dhóid chun éirligh.*[24]

Seán Ó Conaill saw his namesake with sword in hand amid the corpses of his enemies:

> Ag tarraingt a chlaíomh le linn an ghábhaidh
> Na conablaigh sínte do bhíd ar lár.†[25]

Raftery, the blind poet of the West, displayed a certain belligerence, too, in a poem called "Bua Uí Chonaill"—O'Connell's Victory:

> Atá Turcaigh is Gréagaigh ag gabháil dá chéile
> Agus caillfear na céadtha i bhfus agus thall;
> Aimseoidh Sasanaigh agus Franncaigh a chéile
> Agus lasfaidh Éire le faobhar lann;
> M'impí ar Íosa, Dia hAoine a céasadh
> Nár théigh mé in éag go dtige an t-am
> A mbeidh gach cuid aca ag planncadh a chéile
> Agus go bhfaghmaoid pléisiúr ar "Orangemen".
>
> Gunnaí is lámhach is tinte cnámha
> Beidh againn amárach, agus tá sé in am,
> Ó fuair Ó Conaill buaidh ar a námhaid

And the poor Irish in sheltered meadows,
Seducing beauties under the trees.
And the French will come to help in the morning,
And it will be difficult to oppose them,
And the laws on England will be swept from this place,
The church and the clergy will be free;
The Spaniard will come fiercely, with thousands of warriors,
And will break the chains of the Irish,
And it is time for our Stuart to sit in our harbours,
That's all in store for Ireland though it will be hard won.

* The strong man, Daniel, ready and able,
  And a blood-sword in his hand for slaughter.

† Drawing his sword in the fray,
  Corpses strewn, vanquished.

Aipeochaidh bláith is beidh meas ar chrainn;
I gCondae an Chláir tá uaisle is ard-fhlatha
Ag crathadh lámh is ag déanamh grinn
Acht bog faoi an gcárta go n-ólam sláinte
Na bhfear ó Árainn go hInse Chuinn.*26

A song by an anonymous Munster poet describes O'Connell leading his people into battle:

Chuala fuaim na hadhairce ar Shliabh Gaibhle le guth is greann
Ó Conaill is a mhórshluaite go buacach ag teach anall
Tá bualadh ar shliabh le chéile agus lámhach ar dhá thaobh na habhann
Is a chailín bhig na luachra, sin buaite ar chlanna Gall.†27

The Kerry poet, Diarmaid Ó Sé, was a realist. He saw the wretched people thronging to Kilgarvan to attend one of O'Connell's meetings and the verses he wrote on that occasion showed that he understood the magnitude of the task facing O'Connell and the helplessness of the people the great man led:

A Rí Ghil na Rithe do chruinnigh an dream seo
Is gur minic i dteannta iad ag taxanna a gcrá
Is go bhféachaidh Mac Muire orthu ag titim le hamhgar
Is gan acu mar annlann ach brúscar na trá.‡28

---

* The Turks and Greeks are attacking one another
And hundreds will be lost, near and far;
The English and the French will meet,
And Ireland will light with the edge of blades;
I implore Jesus who was crucified on Friday
Not to let me die until the time comes
For the lot of them to be beating one another,
And until we'll take revenge on Orangemen.

We'll have guns and shooting and bonfires tomorrow,
And it is time,
Since O'Connell gained victory over his enemies
Flowers will bloom and trees will blossom;
In County Clare the nobility
Are shaking hands and celebrating,
So send round the measure and we'll drink the health
Of the men from Aran to Inchiquin.

† I heard the sound of the horn of Sliabh Gaibhle,
O'Connell and his hordes coming over in victory;
The battle rages on the hill, and there's shooting on both sides of the river,
And little girl of the rushes, there's the defeat of the English.

‡ O King of Kings who brought those people together,
A people tormented by taxes so often,
May the Son of Mary help them as they fall from hunger,
Without food, except what the sea gives up.

Many Gaelic songs were, as may be seen from some of the quotations above, naive and bitterly sectarian; as poetry some of them are execrable, but at least the poets sang again with gusto, in contrast to what Seamus Heaney has called "the decadent sweet art" of the poets of the eighteenth century.[29]

Many of the songs about O'Connell in English likewise contain what was thought to be dangerous, seditious material. In the spring of 1831, John Irwin, chief constable of Carrickmacross, County Monaghan, wrote to Major Darcy, the inspector general of the constabulary, reminding him of information and requesting permission to prosecute. Two of the ballads the chief constable thought treasonable were "The Repeal of the Union or The Liberation of Mr. O'Connell" and "Freedom, dear Freedom will Carry the Day". The first ballad contains the lines:

> Rejoice each patriotic brother,
> Daniel's foes have knuckled down,
> Freedom's cause will shortly smother
> Tyranny i·. Europe round.[30]

The second song contained the threat:

> But think upon Belgium, sweet Poland and France,
> Where despotic knaves they soon found their graves.[31]

Perhaps what irked Mr. Irwin most was a couplet that suggests that following King Dan's victory:

> Placemen and police must soon go away
> With corporate despots to go and hawk pisspots.[32]

In the same year the police at Newbridge, County Kildare, attempted to stop the public singing of a ballad that contained the vain hope that "Bony and O'Connell will set old Ireland free". This ballad was described as "a most mischievous and seditious libel" and the man who insisted that the police take action wrote that "the hawkers ought to be apprehended but it will be important not to rest there; every effort ought to be made to find out the printer, and through him the person or persons who compose and promote the circulations of such libels". The ballad singer was sent to jail. Indeed such was the hullabaloo about these ballads that the Government deemed it necessary to enforce the 50th of George III, under which a strolling ballad singer might be arrested and committed to prison or the House of Correction until securities could be furnished for his or her good behaviour, or until he or she should be discharged by the magistrate. The law had little effect. The seditious ballads about O'Connell continued to be made, printed and sung. There were innocuous ballads made too, of course. "The Green Flag" is a typical example of the type composed to commemorate O'Connell's meetings. This is part of it:

> Emancipation, he has got,
> He has gained that glorious battle,
> With noble Sheil our worthy friend,
> They'll make the House to rattle,
> So Irishmen join heart and hand,
> I speak to each communion,
> And bravely join the noble Dan
> For to repeal the Union.
> Recorded then it shall be,
> And appear in future story,
> The day O'Connell he was chaired
> In triumph through Kilgory.
> Long live our good and gracious Queen
> Who granted the Reform;
> Success to Dan, that worthy man
> Who does our Isle adorn.
> Our shamrock gay on Patrick's day
> We'll wear in pomp and glory,
> And brave O'Connell wore the same
> When chairing through Kilgory.[33]

There are some amusing ballads concerning O'Connell's skills as a lawyer. The following is part of one called "O'Connell and the Irish Tinkers in London":

> When Daniel O'Connell first went to London
> He then did claim as a member for Clare
> The Cockneys all eager they crowded around him
> And the cheers of our Irishmen rended the air.
> One day through the streets as brave Dan was walking
> A party of Cockneys to view him they stood
> In order to humbug the monarch of Ireland
> One pulled out a note and said, "Sir, is that good?"
> To answer the question brave Dan was not lazy,

> The note to his fob he conveyed in a trice,
> When asked to return he says to the fellow
> "Sir, I'm a counsellor, pay for th' advice!" [34]

There is a hilarious macaronic song about a young man who claimed that creasa an tSamhraidh—the sparks of Summer—led him astray. He was apprehended by the police in Inisteogue, Co. Kilkenny, in broad daylight, pleasuring a young lady in a lane. As he departs for a long stretch at hard labour, he exults:

> But the voice of O'Connell will gain the Repeal
> Is beidh cailíní óga le fáil ag an saol*
> With no opposition and that without fail
> Is beidh peelers gan saibhreas dá ngárlaigh.†[35]

O'Connell was satirized too, of course. His supposed fondness of the ladies is mentioned in a few songs. The conversation between the Old Woman and the Tinker seems to have been a favourite in Dublin public houses:

> On looking around me I espied a bould tinker
> Who only by chance came a strolling that way
> The weather being fine he sat down beside her
> What news honest man, this old woman did say
> Ah 'tis no news at all ma'am replied the bould tinker
> But the people will wish that he never had been
> 'Tis that damnable rogue, bould Daniel O'Connell
> He's now making children in Dublin be steam.
>
> By this pipe in me mouth then, replied the ould woman,
> And that's a great oath on me soul for to say,
> I'm only a woman but if I was near him,
> I bet you my life 'tis damn little he'd say.
> Sure the people of Ireland 'tis very well known,
> They gave him their earnings tho' needing it bad,
> And now he has well recompensioned them for it
> By taking what little diversion they had.
>
> Long life to your courage, replied the bold tinker,
> And long may you live and have youth on your side,
> And if all th' ould women in Ireland were like you,
> O'Connell could throw his steam engine aside.

---

* And everybody will be able to have young girls.
† And peelers' children shall be destitute.

I think every girl that's in th' ould country,
Should begin making children as fast as they can,
And if ever her majesty wanted an army,
We'd be able to send her as many as Dan.[36]

O'Connell was satirized too by the Orange balladeers of the North. A ballad containing the following lines was printed by Mayne of Belfast, who displayed a singular impartiality in printing vitriolic songs for both the Catholic and Protestant factions:

By the tail on Balaam's ass it will surely come to pass,
That the rebels by the score we will put under
Then all the rebel bells from Rome to Royal Kells,
Will proudly ring out The Boyne Water.
Dan O'Connell he may boast of his great big rebel host,
He can swear they're ten million in number
But half of them you'll find, they are both lame and blind,
But we're the bould Orange heroes of Comber.[37]

Another ballad, printed by Mayne for a Catholic ballad-seller, refers to Orange rioting in the wake of an O'Connellite procession:

It is plain to the world they outstepped the law
To spill Roman blood without proper cause,
If processions should grieve them themselves should throw by
Their parading and walking on the 12th of July...

Long live our good queen I hope she'll protect,
From daylight assasins her Roman subjects
And look now with justice upon our sad case
And check each disturber of the public peace...[38]

In Wexford, O'Connell took his place beside Nelson, Wellington, the Czar of Russia, the King of Poland and such traditional heroes as St George in a Forth mumming play composed on the mid 1830's. The barony of Forth is inhabited by descendants of the settlers who came with Fitzstephen in the Anglo–Norman invasion of 1169, and the people who live there retain many of their medieval customs and traditions. The mumming plays derived from the medieval morality plays, and contain a mixture of heroic declarations and dancing.

Enter Daniel O'Connell:

Here I am, the great O'Connell, from a knightly race I came,
My royal habitation lies in ancient Derrynane.

I am the man they call brave Dan, who stood your friend on all
   occasions
And the first MP that ever sat of the Catholic persuasion.
For my country's wrongs I deeply felt, they filled me with vexation
And our cruel foes for to oppose, I formed an Association.
'Tis certain sure, the Church most pure, should persecution bear,
But the penal yoke was lately broke, by electing me in Clare.
To Parliament straight away I went, in hopes to free our nation,
Wellington and Peel, I made them yield, and grant emancipation.
The Catholic rent I underwent, to break and wreck in twain,
Those tyrant's chains, from off those plains, they bound up with
   disdain,
For thirty-three years, it plain appears, our rights to us denied,
They may regret they have borne away their Union as their pride.
And from that time in chains so were bound, for justice we appealed,
We swore that day that come what may to this we would not yield.
By St Patrick's sons you have laurels won, and been raised to dignity
Our brothers cries you did despise, and our country's misery
So now your cause and penal laws, I'll expel by exhortation,
Those notorious tithes I'll lay aside, or in blood I'll steep the nation.
Your tyranny won't frighten me, nor your hellish emigrations.
Your infernal ends, they stood your friends, if I live I'll free the
   nation.[39]

When the great man died his people mourned him in hundreds of
songs. It is said that over one million copies of a ballad called "Erin's
King", or "Daniel is No More" were sold within a short time in Ireland
and in Britain.

> To Mullaghmast, likewise Tara
> As a modern Moses he led us, you see,
> Though we were pursued by proud and haughty
> In the land of promise he left us free
> A shout is gone from Dingle to Derry
> Along the Boyne, the Liffey and the Nore,
> And all repeat in mournful accents,
> Our noble leader, brave Dan no more.[40]

But without a shadow of a doubt, the most moving tribute to the
great leader was penned by a Clareman, Séamus Mac Cuirtín. It is a
noble poem and it struck an apocalyptic note. It was as if death had
dispersed all the old mythologies leaving a new reality in their place:
the great hunger impending over a leaderless nation.

>Beidh t'fheorainn áilne arís fé cháin
>Ag méirligh fhallsa an imreasáin
>Is sliocht na sean le fuacht is fán
>'Na srutha seolta ar seachrán.*[41]

Gone too was the glorification of war as the Clareman reflected on O'Connell's gigantic achievement.

>Ó Conaill cáidh an flaith gan bhéim
>Ad startha fíor do fuair árd réim
>Fíraon Fodhla bhuaigh gach clú
>Gan chréacht gan chosgar, gan fuiliú.†[42]

What more impressive tribute could have been paid to O'Connell, the greatest of the political folk-heroes of Ireland.

Notes

Abbreviations

D.I.F.   Department of Irish Folklore, University College Dublin.
N.L.I.   National Library of Ireland.
P.R.   Private Recording in the author's possession.

1. Johann Georg Köhl, *Reisen in Ireland*, 1843.
2. Recorded by Seán Ó Muirithe, Baile Mhúirne, Co. Cork, 1974. P.R.
3. Recorded by Seán Ó Muirithe, Baile Mhúirne, Co. Cork, 1974. P.R.
4. Cf. Caoimhín Ó Danachair, *Studia Hibernica*, 1974, p. 41; Lady Gregory, *Kiltartan History Book*, pp 23–4; *Béaloideas XI*, 1941, p. 125.
5. Recorded by Seán Ó Muirithe, Baile Mhúirne, Co. Cork, 1974. P.R.
6. Recorded by Seán Ó Muirithe, Baile Mhúirne, Co. Cork, 1974. P.R.
7. D.I.F. Vol. 858: Peig Sayers.
8. *Béaloideas XIV*, 1944, pp 106–7.
9. D.I.F. Vol. 125, p. 363; Vol. 126, p. 207; *An Claidheamh Soluis* 16/8/1902.
10. D.I.F. Vol. 859, pp 66–80.
11. Recorded by Seán Ó Muirithe, Baile Mhúirne, Co. Cork, 1974. P.R.
12. D.I.F. Vol. 125, p. 360.

---

* Your beautiful lands will again be under the yoke
Of false, evil troublemakers,
And the heirs of the ancient stock dispersed,
Scattered in their thousands.
† The gentle O'Connell, the peerless leader,
Who achieved the highest renown,
A good man of Ireland who won every honour
Without a wound, without destruction, without spilling blood.

13. Cf. Caoimhín Ó Danachair, *Studia Hibernica*, 1974, p. 52. The Irish sentence means: Daniel, how would you kill a pig at home?

14. D.I.F. Vol. 485. p. 148.

15. *Béaloideas XI*, 1941, p. 116. This translation is by Seán Ó Súilleabháin, *The Folktales of Ireland*, London 1966.

16. Recorded by Mrs. Mary Sweeney, Meenbanad, Dungloe, Co. Donegal 1960. P.R.

17. Pádraig Ó Míleadha, *Trí Glúine Gaedheal*, Dublin 1953.

18. D.I.F. Vol. 308, p. 239.

19. Caoimhín Ó Danachair, *Studia Hibernica*, 1974, p. 64.

20. Recorded by Thomas Dee, Ardmore, Co. Waterford, 1974. P.R.

21. D.I.F. Vol. 304, p. 44.

22. In imitation of a famous epigram of Swift's, the poet Niall Sheridan composed the following, to add definition to a story concerning O'Connell's last will and testament. James Joyce was fond of quoting it:

> Dying, he left his heart to Rome,
> His testicles he left at home,
> And showed by one satiric touch
> No nation needed them so much.

23. Recorded by Seán Ó Muirithe, Baile Mhúirne, Co. Cork, 1974. P.R. Another version in *Béaloideas*, Vol. VII.

24. *Amhráin Thomáis Rua*, ed. J. Fenton, Dublin, 1922.

25. Recited by Ríonach Ní Fhlathartaigh in D.I.F., 1974.

26. *Abhráin agus Dánta an Reachtabhraidh*, Dublin, 1933, ed. Douglas Hyde, p. 122.

27. Recited by Ríonach Ní Fhlathartaigh, D.I.F., 1974.

28. *Diarmuid na Bolgaighe agus a Chomharsain*, Seán Ó Súilleabháin, Dublin, 1933.

29. 'Aisling', by Séamus Heaney. From *North*, Faber and Faber, London 1975.

30. N.L.I.

31. Ibid.

32. Cf. *Ballads and the Law*, G. Ó Dúghaill, Ulster Folklife XIX, 1973.

33. Ibid.

34. Ibid.

35. Ibid.

36. Recited by Frank Harte, Dublin 1975. P.R.

37. Recited by Frank Harte, Dublin 1975. P.R.

38. N.L.I.

39. Manuscript in the possession of Jack Devereux, Kilmore, Co. Wexford. The entire play is printed in *Irish Folk Drama*, Alan Gailey, Dublin 1970.

40. N.L.I. Printed in *Songs of Irish Rebellion*, Zimmerman, Dublin 1967, p. 231.

41. Cf. Pádraig Ó Fiannachta, *Léas ar an Litríocht*, Dublin 1975.

42. Ibid.

5

The Social and Economic Ideas
of O'Connell*

Joseph Lee

A classic Repeal analysis of the economic condition of Ireland concluded that:

> Political economists have been much puzzled to fix on tangible reasons for the widespread misery of Ireland. At one time they will have it that Ireland is not suited for manufactures, and can prosper only as an agricultural country; at another, that her miseries and failures are owing to her troubled spirit and the insecurity of property consequent thereon; at another, all mischief must be owing to excessive population; then again, the religion of the people is arraigned as the sole cause of their poverty—with a thousand other equally wild and fallacious theories; while almost universal Ireland proclaims, that all her woes and miseries are owing to the hateful Union...[1]

Rarely has the political interpretation of economic history been so categorically affirmed. O'Connell held as an article of faith that Ireland enjoyed unprecedented prosperity under Grattan's Parliament, that the Union brought economic disaster, and that only the restoration of an Irish parliament would revive prosperity.

O'Connell's diagnosis of, and prescription for, Irish socio-economic ills seem clear. Problems arise, however, when one examines the policies he envisaged a Repeal Parliament pursuing. The logical inference of the Repeal view that the abolition of protective duties after the Union exposed Irish industry to overwhelming English competition was that a Repeal Parliament would re-impose protection, under which Irish industry would once again flourish. In contrast to most Repealers, O'Connell did not draw this conclusion, but remained instead wedded to free trade. How then did he anticipate Repeal stimulating economic development?

* This paper could not have been written but for advice and help far beyond conventional scholarly obligation from Professors R.D. Edwards and M.R. O'Connell.

The only major measure he consistently contemplated a Repeal Parliament adopting was a reduction in taxation. This would presumably have led to even less government intervention, if only for lack of money. He assumed that the increased wealth in the pockets of the people would stimulate industrial investment. He did not consider that reduced taxation might augment capital mainly in the hands of classes who did not normally invest in industry. Nor did he ask why, in the absence of protection and with falling transport costs consequent on the steamship and later the railway, capital should invest in Irish rather than British industry. He did assume that Repeal would indirectly promote development by bringing absentee landlords flocking back to Ireland, who would then in turn increase employment by spending their rents at home.

It was not until 1845, however, that he formulated a coherent agricultural programme. Then he demanded the legalisation of the Ulster Tenant Right, compensation for improvements, an absentee tax, compulsory conacre on pasture holdings over 200 acres, reclamation of waste land with a view to the eventual creation of peasant proprietors on it, the breaking up of crown estates into small lots to be sold to the tenants, county agricultural schools, the encouragement of public works through grants as well as loans, and the revision of existing ejectment legislation in favour of the tenant.[2]

This was the most radical land reform programme proposed by any major public figure at that date. The next year, under the impact of the Famine and his fear of social revolution, O'Connell committed himself more firmly to fixity of tenure.[3] This still fell short of the peasant proprietorship that became the popular demand in later generations. Peasant proprietorship, however, would have been in many respects more a conservative than a radical measure before the Famine, when a high proportion of the rural population held no land. O'Connell's compulsory conacre clauses made some attempt, however tentative, to cater for the labourers.

Even in 1846 O'Connell's land policy reflected his faith in the virtues of a resident gentry. The proposed structure for a Repeal Parliament in 1840—reputedly drawn up exclusively by himself[4]—made particular provision for resident landlords.[5] His concept of the role of the resident landlord in Irish society partly reflected his desire to reassure Protestants about the social respectability of Repeal, partly his apparently genuine conviction that landlords needed only to be resident to be good, and partly perhaps, the realisation that resident landlords provided the only realistic administrative alternative to the bureaucratic centralisation that in principle he so disliked.

Apart from his 1845-6 proposals, O'Connell's prescription for economic growth did not differ greatly from the actual policies pursued by Westminster. The Great Famine exposed not only the bankruptcy of government policy but the irrelevance of O'Connell's own approach. Despite his frantic pleas for massive intervention to prevent starvation in 1846 he continued to view large-scale government involvement as an emergency measure, without pausing to ponder whether the emergency might have been averted by more appropriate policies.

The socio-economic challenge of O'Connell's day, however, was enormous. If he failed to suggest realistic solutions, or even to correctly identify some causal connections, it is scarcely for later generations, who have failed to solve simpler problems, to indict him. It is more instructive to simply enquire into the nature and limits of O'Connell's thinking on socio-economic issues to see if they cast light on what manner of man he was.

O'Connell drew political inspiration from four sources—Gaelic, patriot, Benthamite and Catholic. None of the four offered the same sustenance in the social and economic spheres as in the political. His Gaelic heritage included no tradition of systematic social thought. Whatever its cultural riches, Gaelic Ireland flung its children intellectually naked into the world of modern social and economic change. The patriot tradition proved equally barren. Its main contribution was semantic confusion. No Irish leader has subscribed more passionately than O'Connell to the idea of progress, but his vocabulary remained incongruously rooted in historical imagery. No romantic nationalist relied more heavily on the rhetoric of re-incarnation, as O'Connell demanded the restoration of Grattan's Parliament, the revival of Irish industry. He drew his liberalism from quite different sources, but he does not seem to have disciplined his history by his theory, or his theory by his history. In one breath, he attributed economic decay to the Union; in the next, to excessive wage rates due to trade union pressure. He refrained from resorting to anything more demanding than false analogy to reconcile these conflicting explanations.[6] He couldn't even dredge up a false analogy to refute the critics who urged that in Irish circumstances his support for repeal of the Corn Laws on theoretical grounds was incompatible with his support for small farms on historical grounds.

O'Connell often spoke, at least to Bentham, as if Benthanism moulded his socio-economic views. He declared himself a Benthamite on Irish platforms, and even demanded Bentham's forbidding tomes for holiday reading, though how far he waded through the quagmire of Bentham's prose remains doubtful.[7] Bentham's disciples in Britain generally concentrated on restricting government intervention, which they felt was obstructing economic growth. As a result, Benthamism came to be popularly associated with the laissez-faire doctrines attributed to the classical political economists, though this over-simplified the theoretical position of both schools. On the other hand, as industrialisation not only solved old social problems but created new ones, many Benthamites came to demand an interventionist social policy. However intimately Benthamism became associated with particular policies in practice, it is clear that in principle it remained more a technique of thinking than a set of policy prescriptions. To accept O'Connell at his own valuation as a Benthamite does not suffice to explain why he chose particular policies from the range that could be justified by the Benthamite criterion of the greatest happiness of the greatest number.

The problem becomes more intriguing when it emerges that O'Connell rejected the dominant Benthamite/classical economist opinion on several central issues. "The first victory of the Benthamites", as Halevy called the New Poor Law, found O'Connell among the defeated in 1834. Four years later, he defied the bulk of classical opinion in opposing the Irish Poor Law. He refused to worship with the economists at the shrine of the gold standard, advocating instead a silver standard and a bigger currency issue. Despite the pronouncements of the economists, O'Connell persisted in denouncing absenteeism as the principal economic problem of rural Ireland.[8] Far from accepting the conventional contemporary wisdom that Ireland was over-populated, he asserted that she was grossly under-populated in relation to her potential resources. If only these were properly exploited, she could support, in his view, over thirty two million people.[9] His rejection of Malthusian assumptions enabled him dismiss the favourite panacea of the classical economists for Irish improvement, the conversion of small into large farms. Whatever Benthamism and classical economic doctrine may have contributed to O'Connell's socio-economic philosophy, his policy prescriptions reveal him as an incorrigible eclectic by conventional contemporary criteria.

So pragmatic a politician might be expected to sacrifice social and economic principles to political expediency. There is evidence that he was indeed diplomatically absent from some awkward divisions in the House of Commons,[10] and that he vacillated—though within fairly narrow limits—on the factory legislation associated with Ashley, Althorp and Poulett Thompson during the 1830s, depending on how badly a relatively congenial government needed his votes.[11] His vacillations on the Irish Poor Law also owed something to immediate political pressures, but in the end he defied what he took to be Irish opinion by opposing the bill.[12] Hostile Irish opinion did not deter him from supporting free trade. Indeed, the intensity of his liberalism often left him ideologically isolated within his own movement. His tail wagged only feebly on a host of non-Irish issues ranging from his opposition to compensation for West Indian slave owners[13] to his relatively sympathetic attitude towards the Charter.[14] In view of the severe limitations imposed by parliamentary circumstances on his room for manoeuvre, the surprising thing about O'Connell is not that he compromised so much but that he pursued principle inconveniently far on matters of little moment to his Irish constituents.

Self-interest provides no more complete explanation than political opportunism for his social and economic policies. He did, it is true, originally oppose the reversion to the gold standard partly because of the damaging impact on his rents at a moment of personal financial embarrassment.[15] But he continued to sympathise with the silver standard long after his financial situation improved, and he supported Cayley's motion for an enquiry into the currency in 1835.[16] The fear that his rents might suffer did not suffice to sap his support for free trade in butter. His abortive amendment to the Irish Poor Law Bill, to the effect that landlords should pay the whole poor rate, instead of only half, presumably militated against his own self-interest as a landlord.[17]

As a landlord, indeed, he displayed unusual solicitude for his tenants. He scolded his agent, John Primrose, in 1830: "I am sorry you did not give more than £20 to the poor. If they are starving near Derrynane, kill some sheep or a cow and give them and the calves—as they are produced—I would not rear one while the people want the flesh and the milk."[18] When cholera threatened Iveragh he urged Primrose to spare no expense: "I would spend my last shilling rather than not have every possible precaution taken."[19] When the potato crops partially failed in 1839 O'Connell sent £200 worth of potatoes from London to Derrynane with the injunction to "use them discreetly and they will serve to keep down the markets. Give of course as much as needful in charity and, for the rest, get from those who can pay a moderate price. Especially take care to give the people seed."[20] He continued to evince the same intense concern during the Great Famine.[21]

Neither of the obvious explanations, then, opportunism or self-interest, adequately accounts for O'Connell's eclecticism. It may be that he simply didn't understand certain aspects of the economic theories he invoked. He justified his demand for security of tenure on the grounds that

> It was a universal principle in political economy, that where the supply was less than the demand of the article, the price became unnatural, and land was subject to that rule along with other articles. Now, in Ireland the demand for land was greater than the supply, and the price was not natural.[22]

This breath-taking travesty of price theory, if O'Connell really meant it, shakes confidence in his grasp of the most elementary economics. There is little reason to suppose that most nineteenth century politicians, however tightly they clutched at congenial propositions, understood the reasoning of contemporary economics any better than politicians today. Nevertheless, while some genuine misunderstandings may have provided O'Connell with convenient theoretical justification, they cannot account for the range of his deviations from orthodoxy.

Whatever his difficulties at the more recondite theoretical levels, his attitude towards all socio-economic issues reflected a fundamental commitment to the liberty of the individual. This idealism inspired his denunciation of discrimination on grounds of creed, colour and even sex. Government in his view ranked among the greatest oppressors of individuals, and he cast a jaundiced eye at attempts to augment the power of the state. His opposition to the Irish Poor Law arose partly from the powers it vested in officials. He criticised in particular the provisions for emigration, not only because he denied the existence of a population problem, but because the emigration clause granted 'a frightful power' to officials, who could place 'every kind of difficulty and hardship in the way of those they wanted to persuade to emigrate'.[23] The same impulse lay behind his criticism of Peel's income tax on the grounds that it gave the state excessive power to pry into private affairs.[24]

A similar reluctance to countenance restrictions on individual liberty informed O'Connell's approach towards the working classes. To O'Connell, "the worker's property is his labour ... there is not in the world a more rightful property. His title is infinitely beyond that derived from the casualties of modern descent or the chances of ancient plunder."[25] Nevertheless, O'Connell has been bitterly denounced for hostility to the working classes. Critics like James Connolly condemn his allegedly callous indifference to the sufferings of factory children, and his hostility to trade unionism. On the first issue, the critics tend to cite in their support O'Connell's opposition to Ashley's motion in 1838 to amend the order of the day in the House of Commons to deal with violations of the Factory Acts limiting the working hours of children.[26] This overlooks the fact that the motion Ashley attempted to postpone concerned the Irish Tithes Bill, the tardy response to a long agitation in Ireland. The vote on Ashley's motion had as much to do with tithes as with factory children, and it is hardly surprising that O'Connell should have betrayed impatience at Ashley's intervention at this particular juncture. On the substantive issue, O'Connell's reasoning was more complex than his critics allow. He did not pretend, with the normal employer, that the workers had little to complain about. On the contrary, he wished to limit, in an ideal society, not only the working hours of children but also those of adults, "for they were ·overworked".[27] Shorter hours would, however, in his view expose industry to ruinous foreign competition, and lead to even worse unemployment in what was already a bitter slump year. O'Connell's conclusion may have been wrong, but he made no attempt to disguise the existence of suffering, and simply argued that the cure would be worse than the disease.

Connolly further denounced O'Connell as "the most bitter and unscrupulous enemy of trade unionism Ireland has yet produced". O'Connell did not actually condemn trade unionism in principle. On the contrary, he defended the right of workers to form unions, and denounced the Combination Laws which discriminated against labour's right to combine.[28] At this point he drew the line, and proceeded to criticise four basic principles of Dublin craft unionism—the limitation on the number of apprentices, the closed shop, the high entry fines to non-Dublin workers, and the minimum wage. All these measures restricted, in his view, the rights of the individual. Despite his distaste for these restrictions, however, he reserved his real reprobation for attempts to coerce individuals to join unions. He did not denounce the unions until the outbreak of a wave of intimidation, including murder, which some Dublin trade unionists resorted to against both employers and other workers in the slump of 1837-38.[29] O'Connell's genuine hatred of violence did not make exceptions for trade unionists, whom he felt should rely, as should everyone else, on moral instead of physical force.

The basic principles of the Dublin craft unions make it clear that their interests cannot be equated with those of the Irish working classes. Dublin unions represented only a minority of better-off workers. Their regulations were designed to preserve their position not only against employers but against other workers. Their standard of living may have been declining, but in absolute terms it remained far higher than that of the Irish masses. It was therefore scarcely surprising that they opposed the Poor Law, which might have required some financial sacrifice from their members on behalf of the real poor.[30] These unions remained islands of privilege in a sea of working class poverty. It is ironic that James Connolly, who suffered from the resentment of similar unions, should have sprung to their defence. Few of O'Connell's strictures would have applied to the general unions championed by Connolly, who may have anachronistically equated the circumstances of the 1830s with those of his own day.

O'Connell acknowledged the difficulties of craft unionists, never mind the real poor. He argued, however, that restrictive practices only made matters worse for workers as well as employers in the long run.

Wages, which were the price of labour, must depend upon the demand... How was the demand to be created? There was but one way... It was only to be created by tempting capitalists to the country, in order that having cheap labour they might have profits from it. The misfortune of Ireland was, that workmen, impatient of their present state of suffering, did not wait for a gradual and progressive improvement, but they endeavoured by a monopoly to obtain that which ought to arise from the competition of employers.[31]

O'Connell's reasoning about the evolutionary road to economic development through comparatively cheap labour remains theoretically contentious. He was probably wrong in contending that the restrictive practices were ruining several Dublin industries. By this stage union intransigence was as much a consequence as a cause of economic depression. Nevertheless, O'Connell rightly realised that industrialisation offered the only long term solution to Irish poverty. But he was not blind to the human cost of industrialisation. He would have preferred the old domestic system, were it any longer practicable, to the "crowding into pestilential manufactures".[32] He welcomed, if a trifle sceptically, Robert Owen's cooperative experiment in Ireland.[33] He lamented that the working classes were "borne down by the double effects of increasing machinery on the one hand and undiminished taxation on the other".[34] He joined the London Workingmen's Association, which strove to improve working class conditions through education. He supported certain Chartist principles, and made abortive attempts to rally "moral force" Chartists against their "physical force" brethren.[35] He denounced physical force Chartists, not only because of their violence, but because they alienated moderate opinion by identifying reform with revolution and "nearly ruined the cause they professed to advocate".[36] Despite his hatred of violence he petitioned for clemency for the Chartist rebels taken at Newport.[37] He was, then, generally sympathetic to the claims of the under-privileged, provided they were pursued peacefully, and did not involve, in their turn, infringement of basic human rights, as he understood them. Although he never approved closed shop principles, he refrained from denouncing the Dublin unions once violence subsided after 1838.[38] It seems little more logical to claim that he was hostile in principle to the working classes because he denounced trade union outrages than to claim he was hostile to religion because he denounced sectarian outrages, or that he was hostile to the peasantry because he denounced agrarian outrages.

It is difficult to imprison O'Connell within the conventional boundaries of class thinking. Even his solicitude for resident landlords did not derive from any close sense of class solidarity. There were few more scathing critics of aristocratic class selfishness than O'Connell. Few direct representatives of manufacturing interests advocated free trade more passionately or rivalled his scorn for landlord defence of the Corn Laws. He suggested a tax on landed property instead of Peel's income tax, which he felt penalised rising talent.[39] He subscribed in many respects to what Harold Perkin has christened "The Entrepreneurial Ideal".[40]

The entrepreneurial ideal transcended class distinctions. It conferred a moral superiority on the achiever. It was this aura of moral integrity that essentially attracted O'Connell to Benthamism. Utility challenged privilege. Merit challenged monopoly. "Monopoly" ranked next to "Orange" in O'Connell's rich vocabulary of vituperation. To some extent his attitude reflected his own experience in the legal world. His legendary success in his knock-about role as Counsellor tends to divert attention from his unusually gifted legal mind. But political discrimination prevented him reaching the peaks of his profession. He felt a fierce frustration when he measured his rivals against himself, and found them wanting—only to see them achieve the professional recognition denied to him as they slithered their way to legal preferment through political patronage.[41]

In another sense too, O'Connell's legal experience reinforced his reforming resolve. The exploitation of the poor by creatures who bore "the miserable taint of the lawyer craft"[42] intensified his ambition to obtain "a government which will render law, clear and simple in its enactments, and justice cheap and expeditious",[43] a goal that would prove even more elusive than Repeal itself. The discriminatory legal system impressed on the poor that "it is not the justice of the case that is decided before the Magistrate, but the person who has the most favour and interest".[44] The poor naturally responded accordingly. O'Connell strove to elevate popular standards of morality, but he realised the effort was hopeless until the objective grounds for the suspicion were eliminated. Until that happy consummation, bribery and perjury would flourish.

It is in this context that O'Connell's Catholicism emerges as the crucial control on his Benthamism. "The greatest happiness of the greatest number" provides no guide to policy in the absence of a criterion of happiness. Bentham would measure happiness in terms of utility. But Bentham provided no truly independent criterion of utility.

O'Connell did—the natural law. It was the duty of government to create conditions conducive to the functioning of the natural law. It was therefore as a law reformer that O'Connell most specifically proclaimed himself a Benthamite.[45] Bentham's ambition to simplify the legal system would reduce occasions for perjury. Perjury ranked next to murder in O'Connell's league table of immorality. He remonstrated with the incorrigible Pierce Mahony: 'I would not for all the elections in Ireland have one man take the bribery oath falsely... *We must not be bribers.*"[46] A strong argument for the secret ballot was that it would reduce bribery and perjury at elections.[47] He reacted violently to the rumour that the bastardy clauses of the Old Poor Law were to be extended to Ireland partly because of the incitements to perjury they proffered.[48]

Catholic social teaching consisted of little more than commending charity and preaching the integrity of the family. O'Connell clung to both principles. Though he cited the conventional laissez-faire objections to the Irish Poor Law, he rested his case more on moral than on economic grounds.[49] The Poor Law, he believed, 'would be calculated to diminish self-reliance, to paralyse industry, to decrease economy, and above all, to damp and extinguish the kindly and generous feelings of nature towards parents, children, relatives and friends'.[50]

O'Connell derived his concept of the family from natural law. His concept of natural law, in turn, was rooted in a religious morality, reinforced by his own intense family feeling, rather than in the Benthamite "set of generalisations deduced from recurrent natural phenomena".[51] In so far as personal motives influenced O'Connell's response to the Poor Law they probably derived more from his self-image as father and husband, further accentuated by his wife's death in 1836, than from his self-interest as a landlord.

His attitude to the New Poor Law illustrates the relative importance of economic and moral arguments in O'Connell's mind. He detested the Old Poor Law. Far from impugning, with John Walters, the Poor Law Commissioners' use of evidence,[52] he naively commended the integrity of the Commissioners, "a body of men incapable of deception, who could have no possible motive for deceiving parliament...".[53] He pronounced the Report's economic reasoning impeccable: "If ever there was a book of authority published on any subject, it was this report."[54] He castigated Cobbett's defence of the Old Poor Law, even as originally envisaged in the 43rd Eliz., never mind in its allegedly debauched Speenhamland form.[53] Nevertheless, the actual division found him in the same lobby as the much maligned Cobbett—voting against the New Poor Law,[54] "because it did away with personal feelings and connections, because it erected an unconstitutional tribunal, and because it gave an accumulation of votes to the wealthy over the poorer classes".[57] Despite subsequent verbal vacillations, his voting record remained consistent with these principles. He opposed the renewal of the New Poor Law in 1842,[58] just as he had opposed the Irish Poor Law in 1838, when he vainly proposed both one-man-one-vote[59], and the secret ballot, for board of guardian elections.[60]

O'Connell approached free trade from the same moral perspective. His reply to Lord Shrewsbury, who was attempting to mobilise a Catholic vote agains the Repeal of the Corn Laws, reveals that his vigorous sense of Catholic social teaching reinforced his indignation at the injustice inherent in monopoly. To O'Connell, the Corn Laws stood condemned because they raised the price of the poor man's bread to fill the pockets of wealthy agriculturalists. The vigour with which he assailed Shrewsbury reflects his belief that this exploitation was fundamentally incompatible with Catholicism, which "was ever the promoter of every species of charity".[61] He bitterly rebuked Shrewsbury for throwing the Catholic religion "into the scale of the rich and the lordly, against the lowly and the poor".[62] Though he readily invoked the conventional economic arguments against protection, he saw free trade as essentially a moral issue.

Many politicians have professed their faith in the natural law. A few have been as genuinely devout as O'Connell. He was, however, unusual among major Irish public figures in refusing to draw a convenient distinction between private and public morality. No Irish public figure since his time has tried to impose on himself, or on his people, such demanding moral standards. He would not barter or truck with his God. He would not even create his God in his own image. This lack of moral elasticity, all the more striking in so tactically agile a politician, induced him to brand almost all killing as murder, however subjectively sacred the cause. "The moment", he reproached Dublin trade unionists, "they attempted to coerce others ... that instant crime commenced, and they were not only guilty of a crime in the eye of the law, but also of a moral crime ... ."[63]

He condemned slavery basically on the simple grounds of Christian morality, "to do to others as we would they should do to us".[64] Nor did he seek refuge in the fashionable sophistry that this merely meant that slave holders should treat their slaves as they themselves would wish to be treated—if they were slaves! Consistently in the context, the only compromise in principle he was prepared to contemplate in his free trade convictions was to achieve a higher moral good. He objected to the equalisation of the sugar duties between the slave owning sugar planters outside the British colonies and the sugar producers in the colonies whose slaves had recently been emancipated, on the grounds that access to the British market on equal terms would benefit the slave owners. "I would not consent to give the people of England, or of Ireland either, cheap sugar at the expense of robbery and stealing. And I will not consent to give it to them by the murder of the Negro."[65] O'Connell may have momentarily faltered on this issue, for there is some evidence that he pressed his objections more vigorously against Peel than he had earlier against Melbourne. But there is no reason to doubt the intensity of O'Connell's moral commitment on the matter. It was on the same principle that, at a much more mundane level, he showed himself oblivious to the morality of the market place by refusing to sell sick sheep for fear of spreading disease.[66]

O'Connell, then, felt intense commitment to his version of Catholic social teaching. His Benthamism was essentially ethical rather than doctrinal, and there was more to his philosophy of happiness than the felicific calculus dreamt of. Why he chose to interpret Catholic doctrine in this particular manner raises interesting issues, which remind us just how little we know about the religion of this remarkably religious man.

His Catholicism may have conditioned O'Connell's approach to socio-economic issues in one other respect. The primacy of moral criteria in his thinking may help account for his failure to make adequate allowance for regional differences. The Famine brutally exposed the existence of a number of more or less independent economies within Ireland, including the existence of a separate Lagan Valley economy. O'Connell always adopted a cavalier attitude towards the implications of Belfast economic growth for his political interpretation of Irish economic history. He bitterly lamented the alleged decline of the linen industry—which he imputed to the Union, of course—at a moment when that industry had begun to recover impressively from the difficulties of the Napoleonic Wars. If O'Connell originated the tradition of dogmatic nationalist ignorance of east Ulster, with its insistence on sacrificing the Belfast economy to southern interests, he could plead genuine ignorance as an excuse. Closer to home, however, he was familiar with three types of economies—agricultural Iveragh, commercial Dublin, industrial England. Yet he insisted on applying the same socio-economic doctrines to Derrynane, Dublin and Manchester. He did not relate policies to stages of economic development. He thought of economic and social measures more in terms of right and wrong than in terms of economic and social theory. Partly because he thought in unchanging moral terms, his social and economic thinking underwent little development over a forty-year period, despite the rapidly changing relative positions of the British and Irish economies, and of regional economies within Ireland. The universalism of his Catholicism subordinated the intrinsic relativities of socio-economic issues to moral absolutes, which transcended time and place.

Unfortunately, family solidarity and charity proved no more effective barriers to famine than the free functioning of market forces. As the poor increased and multiplied and filled the Irish earth, charity was not enough, if only because there could not be enough charity. Whatever the spiritual riches of the Catholic tradition, intellectually it could provide no solution to the problem of Irish poverty.

O'Connell had peculiarly difficult personal roles to play. If in Derrynane he incarnated the traditional qualities of the Gaelic chief, to Gladstone he appeared a complete English liberal. Much though he relished the sporting life at Derrynane, he responded to a different call. In Dublin and London he was very much a self-made man, fanatically ambitious, living laborious days. It was as if he could shed one personality and don another, and feel perfectly at ease in both, without pondering the peculiarity of his position. The problem of O'Connell's personality is that there was no problem. To have been normal, he should have been, at the very least, a schizophrenic! Instead, he seems to have been a supremely integrated individual. It may have been, though here we tread on highly speculative ground, the sense of psychological security he derived from his Catholicism that enabled him bridge enormous culture gaps effortlessly—with the unfortunate corollary that he was never forced to fully face some fundamental questions concerning Irish social and economic development.

O'Connell was not a professional socio-economic theorist. He should not be assessed by standards more appropriate to the study than to the platform. Nevertheless, if his approach to economic matters may have been technically defective, his attitude to social questions was more consistent and more perceptive than might have been surmised, and helps bring the essential O'Connell into clearer focus.

Notes

1. *Report of the Committee of the Loyal National Repeal Association of Ireland, on the disastrous effects of the Union on the woollen, silk and cotton manufactures of Ireland* (Dublin, 1840), p. 108.
2. *First, Second and Third Reports of the . . . Loyal National Repeal Association on the Land Question* (Dublin, 1845), especially the Third Report, pp. 321-26.
3. *Hansard*, LXXXVII, 377.
4. W.J. O'Neill Daunt, *Personal Recollections of Daniel O'Connell* (London, 1848), I, p. 152.
5. *The Report of the Committee of the National Association of Ireland . . . for the reconstruction of the House of Commons of Ireland* (Dublin, 1840), p. 51.
6. W.J. O'Neill Daunt, *op. cit.*, I, pp. 21-2.
7. O'Connell to Bentham, 30 July, 22 October 1829, John Bowring (ed.), *The Works of Jeremy Bentham* (Edinburgh, 1843), XI, pp. 20, 22.
8. R.D.C. Black, *Economic Thought and the Irish Questions* (Cambridge, 1960), Ch. 3.
9. Calculated from *Evidence on the state of Ireland* (London, 1825), pp. 141, 190.
10. D.C. Riach, 'O'Connell and Slavery', in D. McCartney (ed.), *The World of Daniel O'Connell* (Dublin, 1980), p. 178.
11. F. D'Arcy, 'O'Connell and the English Radicals', in D. McCartney, *ibid*, p. 69.
12. *Ibid.*, p. 101; A. MacIntyre, *The Liberator* (London, 1965), p. 217.
13. *Hansard*, XX, 206.
14. *Ibid.*, LXIII, 88.
15. M.R. O'Connell (ed.), *The Correspondence of Daniel O'Connell* (Dublin, 1972-1980), II, Letter 959, O'Connell to his wife, 6 May 1822. Hereafter cited as *O'Connell Corr.*
16. *Ibid.*, III, no. 1297, O'Connell to W.C. Plunkett, 7 March 1826; IV, Letter 1662a, O'Connell to the Knight of Kerry, 7 April 1830; V, Letter 2245, O'Connell to Edward Ellice, 11 May 1835; *Hansard*, XVII, 586, XXVIII, 338. See F.W. Fetter, *Development of British monetary orthodoxy* (Cam-

bridge, Mass., 1965), pp. 139-43, 164.

17. *Hansard*, XL, 979.
18. O'Connell to John Primrose, Jr., 7 July 1830, *O'Connell Corr.*, IV, Letter 1691.
19. Same to same, probably 1 March 1834, *ibid.*, V, Letter 2047.
20. Same to same, 15 March 1839, *ibid.*, VI, Letter 2595.
21. O'Connell to Maurice O'Connell, 1 June, 27 August 1846, *ibid.*, VIII, Letters 3223 and 3271.
22. *Hansard*, XLI, 983.
23. *Ibid.*, XLI, 377-8.
24. *Ibid.*, LXII, 407.
25. D. O'Connell, *Observations on Corn Laws, on political probity and ingratitude, and on clerical and personal slander; in the shape of a meek and modest reply to the second Letter of the Earl of Shrewsbury, Waterford and Wexford* (Dublin, 1842), p. 6.
26. James Connolly, *Labour in Ireland* (Dublin, n.d.), p. 124.
27. *Hansard*, XLIII, 978.
28. *Ibid.*, 1085.
29. F.A. D'Arcy, 'The artisans of Dublin and Daniel O'Connell, 1830-47: an unquiet liaison', *Irish Historical Studies*, XVII, No. 66 (September 1970), pp. 227-39; Patrick Holohan, 'Daniel O'Connell and the Dublin Trades: a Collision, 1837-8', *Saothar: Journal of the Irish Labour History Society*, Vol. I, No. 1 (May 1975), pp. 1-17.
30. MacIntyre, *op. cit.*, p. 217.
31. *Hansard*, XL, 1086-7.
32. Daniel O'Connell, *Letters on the Repeal of the Legislative Union between Great Britain and Ireland* (Dublin, 1830), IV, p. 31.
33. O'Connell to his wife, 18 April 1823, *O'Connell Corr.*, II, Letter 1010; to J.K. Johnston, 10 May 1823, *ibid.*, Letter 1019.
34. O'Connell to G.J. Harney, 24 December 1837, *O'Connell Corr.*, VI, Letter 2485a.
35. J.H. Treble, 'O'Connor, O'Connell and the attitudes of Irish Immigrants towards Chartism in the north of England 1838-48' in J. Butt and I.F. Clarke (eds), *The Victorians and social protest* (Newton Abbott, 1973), n. 17, p. 221.
36. *Ibid.*, p. 38.
37. O'Connell to James Martin, 4 February 1840, W.J. Fitzpatrick, *Correspondence of Daniel O'Connell* (London, 1888), pp. 222-3.
38. D'Arcy, *op. cit.*, pp. 239 *et seq.*
39. *Hansard*, LXII, 402-408.
40. Harold Perkin, *The origins of modern English society 1780-1880* (London, 1969), pp. 221-30.
41. See also O. MacDonagh, 'O'Connell in the House of Commons', in D. Mac Cartney (ed.), *op. cit.* p. 44.
42. O'Connell to T. Lyons, 28 September 1840, *O'Connell Corr.*, VI, Letter 2751.

43. O'Connell to W.S. Crawford, 17 September 1834, *O'Connell Corr.*, V, Letter 2116.
44. *Evidence on the state of Ireland* (London, 1825), p. 165.
45. O'Connell to Bentham, 30 July 1829, 22 October 1829, *O'Connell Corr.*, VIII, Letters 3413,3416.
46. O'Connell to P. Mahony, 22 July 1837, *O'Connell Corr.*, VI, Letter 2440.
47. *Hansard*, LXII, 941; LXIV, 408.
48. O'Connell to Archbishop Murray, 10 March 1830; to J.K.L., 19 March 1830, *O'Connell Corr.*, IV Letters 1639 and 1653.
49. W.J. O'Neill Daunt, *op. cit.*, I, p. 276.
50. *Hansard*, XL, 948, 951-2.
51. U.R.Q. Henriques, 'Bastardy and the New Poor Law', *Past and Present*, 37 (July 1967), p. 110.
52. See N.C. Edsall, *The Anti-Poor Law Movement, 1834-44* (Newton Abbott, 1971), pp. 15-21.
53. *Hansard*, XVII, 873.
54. *Ibid.*
55. O'Connell to Richard Barrett, 2 October 1834, *O'Connell Corr.*, V, Letter 2117.
56. *Hansard*, XXIV, 1061.
57. *Ibid.*, 1060.
58. *Ibid.*, LXV, 510.
59. *Ibid.*, XLI, 998.
60. *Ibid.*, 1001.
61. D. O'Connell, *op. cit.*, p. 3.
62. *Ibid.*, p. 4.
63. *Hansard*, XL, 1085.
64. O'Neill Daunt, *op. cit.*, I, p. 284.
65. Quoted in C. Duncan Rice, '" Humanity sold for sugar!": the British abolitionist response to Free Trade in slave grown sugar', *The Historical Journal*, XIII, 1970, p. 414.
66. *O'Connell Corr.*, III, Letter 1383, O'Connell to John Primrose, Jr., 24 April 1827.

6

O'Connell and British Politics

A. D. Macintyre

In his attacks on the men of Young Ireland, Daniel O'Connell spoke of himself as the representative of "Old Ireland". In scoring an effective debating point against his opponents, he spoke more prophetically than he knew. His "Old Ireland" with its huge population, "the nation of eight millions" on which his power rested, died in the Great Famine; and in that catastrophe much of his own work and reputation seemed also to perish. Yet it can still be claimed for him that no other Irishman has exerted so dominant and so continuous an influence on British politics. He established the broad patterns both of Ireland's development and of her place in the British political system. Later Irish leaders—Isaac Butt, Charles Stewart Parnell, John Redmond and Arthur Griffith—were his direct heirs, the heirs of a tradition in which Irish nationalism was fused with British constitutionalism. There are fundamental continuities beneath the divisions of Irish history: of the making of the Free State, J. C. Beckett has perceptively remarked that "the hand was the hand of Collins, but the voice was the voice of O'Connell".[1]

O'Connell brought Ireland into the heart of British politics. The methods which he used—the organization of a series of mass movements to influence Parliament and (after 1830) to support his own actions there—were partly his own invention, partly the result of his working within an existing British tradition of popular politics. His age, often called one of "Improvement", was also and conspicuously an age of "Agitation". Indeed for many liberals, the two terms were virtually synonymous: agitation embodied freedom and created progress. To traditionalists, agitation was a threat to social order and to the sovereignty of Parliament.[2] Other men in O'Connell's time made important contributions to the development of British radicalism: Sir Francis Burdett of Radical Westminster, William Cobbett in his journalism, 'Orator' Hunt, Thomas Attwood of the Birmingham Political

Union, Richard Cobden of the Anti-Corn Law League, Fergus O'Connor the Chartist. But none matched O'Connell's achievement. He was the greatest agitator of his day, and, unlike most other agitators, he also became a great parliamentary leader.

Historians of British politics often misunderstand the British dimensions of O'Connell's career. They see him simply as the personification of "the Irish Question" of his time, that alien force outside the main pattern of British politics violently disturbing and occasionally distorting what would otherwise have produced a smooth and progressive evolution. Halévy reflected this view when he wrote of O'Connell as "the national hero of a foreign people", the leader of an Irish party which was "a species of foreign body lodged in the entrails of the British Parliament".[3] The real situation was more complex and more interesting. The Act of Union created after 1800 a new British political system of which Ireland, with its hundred members in the Imperial Parliament, was an integral part. The Union dominated O'Connell's entire career, but not merely because he opposed it. Indeed he acted at times to make the Union work, as he thought, properly. Parliament gradually but decisively moulded the development of Ireland to carry out a slow, modernizing revolution to which Irish opinions and actions contributed quite as much as English policy. O'Connell's support for reforms obtained through Parliament gave a powerful, probably irreversible momentum to this process. Irish questions might well have seemed foreign to English experience and often produced strong reactions from politicians and public opinion, but they could never be treated as isolated problems. The gradual assimilation between the two countries meant that almost every Irish issue had its British or imperial counterpart. These issues were often fundamental, and on their outcome depended the political future of Great Britain.

Catholic Emancipation, the cause on which O'Connell's career was built, was such an issue. The prime interest of the newly assertive Catholic middle class, of gentry owning or holding land, of lawyers, journalists, merchants, shopkeepers and tenant farmers who demanded a full share in local government and parliamentary representation, Emancipation involved at least a considerable redistribution, perhaps a transfer of power in Ireland.[4] But it was also a British question. The Catholics' case rested on the doctrines, shared alike by Englishmen and Irishmen, of 'the good old cause' of civil and religious liberty. Whig theories which had been used in the seventeenth century to exclude Catholics were now reformulated to support their inclusion. The Whig Macaulay, in his *History of England*, found no difficulty in vindicating the policies of exclusion and inclusion, measures respectively and 'unanimously approved by all the great English statesmen of the seventeenth century... [and] of our own time". Yet if the Catholic claims were to be conceded, they would produce a drastic alteration in the Anglican settlement established by the Revolution of 1688. They were a direct challenge to the constitution, to the organic unity of Church and State, to the whole definition of citizenship. For behind the Irish Catholics were other groups excluded from the political nation: the Protestant dissenters, the new and powerful interests of the unrepresented industrial cities, the mass of the voteless population. If the doors were opened to the Catholics in Ireland, when and how could they be shut again? The Catholic question united the Whig opposition and a growing body of radical reformers in and out of Parliament; it seriously divided the Tory governing coalition under Lord Liverpool whose system depended on his colleagues' and followers' delicate agreement to differ on the question; and by 1825, the pro-Catholic majority in the House of Commons was ranged against the King and the House of Lords. The agitators in Ireland broke this deadlock. O'Connell had created a mass political movement in which the peasantry had been mobilised under clerical and middle-class leadership, and he now turned it against the Irish electoral system with his own victory in the County Clare bye-election in July 1828. His defeated opponent William Vesey Fitzgerald, an amiable landlord and an experienced politician who was himself a supporter of Emancipation, wrote in despair to Robert Peel, the Home Secretary, in London:

> All the great interests broke down, and the desertion has been universal. Such a scene as we have had! Such a tremendous prospect as it opens to us ... The organisation exhibited is so complete and so formidable that no man can contemplate without alarm what is to follow in this wretched country.[5]

To the government, Emancipation now seemed the only alternative to the collapse of Irish society into rebellion and civil war. Wellington and Peel were right to acknowledge the power of the Catholic Association, wrong to see it as a revolutionary movement. It was in fact profoundly reformist. O'Connell's radical aims in politics were matched by conservative views about Irish society. Neither he nor his leading lay and clerical supporters intended to preside over a peasant revolution in the countryside; and the Catholic Association, by stressing the grievances shared by all Catholics and drawing attention in a much more muted fashion to those matters which particularly affected some groups among the peasantry, effectively countered any possible threat from the peasant masses. Thus, the complaints in the petitions and meetings of the Catholic Association about conditions of land tenure, rents, taxation and education, for example, can only have been of concern to those peasants above the subsistence line, to those with some sense of rising expectations. O'Connell's manipulation of the various forces at work within Irish society was always deft and opportunistic, but it was not cynical. His early education, the influence of his family, and his position as a landlord strongly inclined him towards a paternalist and hierarchical conservatism. Yet he had become a liberal during his two years as a law student in London when he read Voltaire, Rousseau, Gibbon, Paine, Godwin and Adam Smith; and the later influence of Bentham's utilitarianism merely gave edge and assurance to an orthodox liberalism which he maintained with passionate conviction all his life.[6] His belief in civil and religious equality and in freedom of conscience and speech under the law naturally aligned him with the English Whigs; his faith in the laws of political economy as enunciated by Smith and refined by Ricardo was shared by Whigs, by most Radicals and by O'Connell's chief Conservative opponent, Peel. Like almost all men of his generation, he drew the lesson from the French Revolution and from the experience of the United Irishmen that armed rebellion was unjustified even in the best of causes. He wanted to rationalize his world, not to revolutionize it.

The Irish Catholic movement drew its political inspiration and most of its methods from many earlier movements, English, Scottish and Irish, which had pressed reforms on Parliament: the agitations associated with John Wilkes, Christopher Wyvill's Association movement during the American war, the Irish Volunteers of Grattan and Charlemont, the campaigns of the English dissenters on the eve of the French Revolution and the successive radical movements, middle class and plebeian, from the early 1790's to the aftermath of the Napoleonic wars. The Catholic Association, with its popular subscriptions, public meetings and petitions, its newspapers and propaganda, was an episode in the history of British radicalism. It differed from other movements only in its tremendous scale and in its special (and especially explosive) Irish context. These differences were important. O'Connell succeeded, where all the other movements had failed, in creating a movement which appealed across the lines of class and religion and which was too powerful to be suppressed by the law. Catholic Emancipation was a great personal triumph for him; it was still more momentous in its consequences for British politics. It completed the disintegration of the old Tory party and weakened the constitutional independence of the Crown and the House of Lords; it undermined the belief of many Englishmen, particularly the vengeful Ultra-Protestant Tories, in the old unreformed system which had capitulated not only to the Catholics but also, by the repeal of the Test and Corporation Acts in 1828, to the Protestant dissenters; and it greatly encouraged those Whigs and Radicals who wanted reform.[7] The Political Unions which were to play a vital part in the crises over the Reform Bill in 1831 and 1832 were founded on the direct model of the Catholic Association.[8] O'Connell himself was a member both of the Metropolitan Political Union (in London) and of Thomas Attwood's much more influential Birmingham Political Union. In May 1829, Attwood declared that "the Irish people have lately obtained a glorious and bloodless victory".[9] Like O'Connell, Attwood aimed at and temporarily achieved a union of the middle and working classes.

In February 1830, O'Connell took his seat as MP for Clare and at once aligned himself with the English Radicals led by Burdett, Hunt and Joseph Hume. By his support for manhood suffrage, triennial parliaments and vote by ballot, free trade, the abolition of slavery and sweeping measures of retrenchment to break the aristocracy's control of patronage, he provided powerful reinforcement to the reformers' campaigns. His parliamentary activities were closely linked with continued agitation in Ireland, where he launched his first campaign for repeal of the Act of Union. In this way, he kept in being the movement which had won Emancipation and coupled it with a programme of immediate reforms: of the electoral system (from which the forty-shilling freehold voters in the counties had been excluded under the Emancipation settlement), the law, local government and tithes.[10] Lord Grey's Whig government, in power after the fall of Wellington in November 1830, failed in their efforts to buy O'Connell off with office, to prosecute him and to suppress his movement. The government's difficulties were increased by the fact that O'Connell played an important and even crucial part in the debates and crises over the Reform Bill. Like other Radicals, he supported the Bill warmly and loyally even though it did not go as far as he wanted. His speeches made it clear that he could dominate the Commons, despite the prejudice of most of its members against him as a reputedly mercenary Irish demagogue, and he was already building up the nucleus of an independent Irish party.

Historians can now see that the Reform Acts of 1832 led to the creation of a two-party system, although one which was neither entirely new nor permanent. This was not obvious to men in 1833. They saw a large but ill-disciplined majority for the Whig ministry, a much smaller and demoralized Tory opposition and, holding the balance, well over one hundred Radicals succinctly described by one Tory as 'Cobbettites and Humeites and Irish blackguards".[11] Many who had supported the Reform Bill must have secretly feared that they had created a monster which would destroy the traditional parties; as the Duke of Richmond put it, "Attwood and O'Connell will turn the scale in the end".[12] So far as Ireland was concerned, the Irish Reform Act, as limited a measure as the Whigs could decently make it, had in fact produced a fairly even party balance. But O'Connell's Repeal party with its well-drilled party machine, funds and newspapers, its use of the influence of the priests against the interests of the landlords, its popular support against an alarming background of agrarian disturbances, emerged as the largest single Irish party with 39 members. United by the pledge (a device beloved by most Radicals) to support Repeal, this party was a new phenomenon. It showed its mettle in opposition to the government's repressive Coercion Bill, which blamed the nationalist movement for agrarian disturbances. In his green frock coat and black, broad-brimmed hat, his "massive figure staggering with rage—the face darkened with all the feelings of scorn and rancour", O'Connell gave his finest parliamentary performance. He had always, he said, condemned agrarian outrages; and if the government suppressed all political activity which he saw as a positive brake on such violence, he prophesied that there would indeed be "a revolution of the sword in Ireland".[13]

For three years, Ireland dictated the course of British politics. Grey's government could not rule Ireland simply by coercion; but in its attempts to conciliate O'Connell and Irish public opinion, particularly by reforms in the tithe system and of the established Church, it gradually broke up, losing first Stanley, Graham, and two other ministers, then, in June 1834, Grey himself. Ireland gave William IV his chance to dismiss Melbourne's administration in November 1834; Peel's first government fell in April 1835 on the issue of Appropriation, by which part of the Church's income was to be set aside for secular purposes in Ireland. O'Connell exploited very skilfully the divisions which Irish questions caused among British politicians and parties. He now held the balance of power, and he used it to introduce political stability. The so-called Lichfield House Compact, the alliance of Whigs, Radicals and the Irish party to overthrow Peel in 1835, created a broad two-party system within which O'Connell acted for six years in alliance with Melbourne's government. His decision was logical and realistic. The overwhelming defeat of his own Repeal motion in the Commons in April 1834 showed conclusively that British parties were immovable on the maintenance of the Union. He hated Peel and the prospect of Tory rule in Ireland; a genuinely liberal government was now committed to and carried out some tangible reforms, including a settlement of the tithe question (although without Appropriation) and the grant of elective councils to Dublin, Belfast and eight other places. For the Whigs, alliance with O'Connell gave them office and greatly eased the problems of governing Ireland. More important, they produced an efficient administration in Ireland which showed itself determined to act in sympathy with the outlook of the majority, opening public office to eligible Catholics and thus fulfilling the promise of Emancipation. Thomas Drummond, the Under-Secretary at the Castle until his death in 1840, is often and rightly described as the moving spirit of the Whig administration in Ireland. But his work would not have been nearly as effective without Lord John Russell's political leadership as Home Secretary, Mulgrave's loyalty and appropriate flamboyance as Lord-Lieutenant and Morpeth's competence as Chief Secretary.

These gains must be set against disadvantages. O'Connell's methods, his commanding position, his political *style*—the ferocious personal attacks on opponents, on Grey whom he called "a wretched old man with a maniacal contempt for the people of Ireland", on "the Saxon" Stanley, on Peel and Wellington, even on the young and relatively obscure Disraeli—aroused deep and general resentment in England. Lashed by O'Connell, *The Times* fought back with constant attacks on the alleged political dangers of Roman Catholicism, on the "O'Connell Cabinet" and on O'Connell himself, who was held up as "scum condensed of Irish bog". Disraeli's personal feud with O'Connell doubtless increased the venom of his attacks, but a political journalist and adventurer such as Disraeli will generally reflect prevailing opinions. In his celebrated open letters in *The Times* published under the pseudonym of "Runnymede", Disraeli described O'Connell as "the hired instrument of the Papacy; as such his mission is to destroy your Protestant society, and, as such, he is a more terrible enemy to England than Napoleon". Disraeli's invective against the Irish, "this wild, reckless, indolent, uncertain and superstitious race" whose "fair ideal of human felicity is an alternation of clannish broils and coarse idolatry", is well described by his modern biographer as displaying that "virulent racial and religious prejudice towards Ireland" which was "one of the least commendable features of Victorian politics".[14] Such attitudes would be beneath contempt and notice if they had not been so general and so representative. Where Disraeli and *The Times* led, others followed. O'Connell's characteristic blend of extremism outside Parliament with relative moderation inside it, was seen as typical of the agitator, of the "Big Beggarman" who appeared to have a personal financial stake in fomenting agitation. His interventions in British affairs did credit to his broad ideas about the duties of a parliamentary leader, but his campaigns in England and Scotland in 1835 and 1836 for an elective House of Lords and his attacks on trades unionism alienated possible allies without conciliating opponents. He stood up for Ireland, but he never made any consistent or considered attempt to persuade English opinion of the justice of Irish demands.

In the resurgence of Conservatism after 1835, the old English tradition of No-Popery, the stock in trade of low journalists and popular preachers, played fully as important a part as Peel's emphasis on a programme of reforms and good electoral organization. Conservatives eagerly capitalised on the rising tide of opposition to Catholicism which was directly related to O'Connell's ascendancy at a time when British society was absorbing a rapidly growing number of Irish immigrants, many of them very poor.[15] O'Connell's parliamentary party, now a coalition of nationalists and liberals, was regarded as a set of office-hungry social upstarts entirely subservient to him, his "Tail" as it was often called. In fact, it was chiefly a party of landlords, Protestant as well as Catholic, men whose economic interests and political morality were not essentially different from those of most other MP's. The party contained a few rascals and adventurers, but it included many more who were honest and public-spirited and some, like Richard Lalor Sheil and William Smith O'Brien, of real distinction. Those, including members of his own family, who accepted office did so with O'Connell's encouragement and, often, on his recommendation. As it was gradually fulfilled, Emancipation undermined the party's political cohesion and independence.

The victory of the Conservatives in the election of 1841 showed the strength of reaction. Established institutions in church and state had survived in most respects unscathed, and radicals had to turn again to agitation out of doors. English radicalism split on increasingly definite class lines: sections of the middle class to pursue free trade through the Anti-Corn Law League, the working classes to demand social reform and political rights in Chartism. O'Connell rebuilt his Repeal movement and led it to a climax of agitation in the huge and orderly meetings of 1843, the Repeal Year.[16] But in thinking that he could repeat the success of 1829, he seriously misjudged the situation. By the 1840's and partly because of the earlier reforms, Parliament was much less responsive to external pressures than it had been in the 1820's; Peel's position was incomparably stronger than Wellington's had been. O'Connell, the Chartists and the Anti-Corn Law League all learnt this lesson. O'Connell, at first a patron of Chartism, would have nothing to do with the movement after it passed into the control of his former rebellious follower Feargus O'Connor and moved, in some regions, towards physical force. He certainly hoped to use the League which had been founded on the model of his own organizations and whose cause he warmly supported: it would, he said optimistically, "compel the aristocracy to yield in England and leave us Ireland to ourselves".[17] But the League's leaders never gave any support to O'Connell's campaign to repeal the Act of Union, although they benefited, notably in their own base of Manchester, from his influence over most of the Irish in Britain. Peel was not simply fighting the battle of the aristocracy, and his decision to repeal the Corn Laws was as much the result of his own developing ideas and policies as of the League's pressure.

O'Connell's movement brought reforms to Ireland, but from the quarter which he detested. Peel's Irish policies—the Devon Commission of enquiry into the Irish land system, the Charitable Bequests Bill, the generously increased Maynooth grant and the Colleges Bill—were his constructive responses to the threat of nationalist agitation. But while they amply demonstrated the weakness of O'Connell's position in Parliament and contributed to the revolt of the Young Irelanders against O'Connell's leadership and methods, these Irish policies seriously damaged Peel's relations with his own supporters. By 1846, famine and fears for public order in Ireland, the issue of Free Trade against Protection, the fate of Peel's government and career were all locked together—a savage epitome of British politics under the Union. In joining the Whigs, Radicals and Tory Protectionists in what Wellington called the "blackguard combination" to bring Peel down, O'Connell and his party made their last contribution. Thereafter they were mere adjuncts of Lord John Russell's Whig government. They were also, for the English public, the representatives of the Irish landlords who were largely if unfairly held to blame for the Famine and must be made responsible for its victims.

O'Connell was now over seventy, and his powerful physique and mind were gradually deteriorating. He made desperate efforts to bring home to Parliament the extent of the disaster in Ireland, but he had little influence on the government's plans. His old enemy Disraeli, whose maiden speech had been drowned by the hisses, hoots and laughter of the Irish members but who now ten years later found himself acting with O'Connell against Peel, wrote a memorable account of one such effort by O'Connell. Speaking for nearly two hours from the place occupied usually by the leader of the Opposition and in a voice audible only to those near him and to ministers, O'Connell presented

> a strange and touching spectacle to those who remembered the form of colossal energy and the clear and thrilling tones which had once startled, disturbed and controlled senates ... To the house generally it was a performance of dumb show, a feeble old man muttering before a table; but respect for the great parliamentary personage kept all as orderly as if the fortunes of a party hung upon his rhetoric.

"Ireland was in their hands", O'Connell said in his last speech in the Commons, "if they did not save her, she could not save herself".[18] Before he died, at Genoa on 15 May 1847 on his way to Rome, he knew how that appeal had been received.

It was not an accident that O'Connell's career ended in an atmosphere of division and failure, when men of a new generation challenged the methods and direction of his leadership. He had built for a time a coherent and disciplined movement which expressed the energies and ideals of most Irish people—as Parnell was later to do. But the achievements of O'Connell and Parnell were exceptions rather than the rule. In the nineteenth and early twentieth centuries, disarray in Irish politics was much more normal than harmony. The cause is to be found in the powerful but indeterminate sense of Irish nationality. Much divided Ireland from Britain, but much also united the two countries. Did Irishmen want independence, or did they want self-government within the Empire? O'Connell sought the second of these alternatives, but later history was to show that his was no settled answer.

Many years after his death, his remarkable contributions to the theory and practice of British politics were recognized. In 1889, Gladstone said of O'Connell that he was "as thorough an English Liberal, as if he had had no Ireland to think of"; but that he was also "the greatest popular leader whom the world had ever seen . . . , who never for a moment changed his end [and] never hesitated to change his means".[19] To Gladstone the Home Ruler, O'Connell was "a prophet of the coming time". O'Connell's end was the rebuilding of Ireland's national life; the means had been the democratic expression of popular rights and interests within the oligarchic framework of representative government. This was to become the British liberal tradition. O'Connell, Gladstone and David Lloyd George were its outstanding exponents. They were practical and flexible politicians; they could express, in their personalities and in their oratory, the ideals which they shared with people of different classes and nationalities. In each man, broad reforming sympathies were balanced by a hard and conservative core. Each was faced in his time by the problem of violence in politics; each showed that he believed in settling divisions by discussion and agreement rather than by the use of force.

Notes

1. J. C. Beckett, "Ireland under the Union", in his *Confrontations: Studies in Irish History* (1972), p. 151. The quotation comes from an essay in which the myths and realities of nineteenth and early-twentieth century Irish history are briefly and brilliantly analysed.

2. In 1867, Gladstone told the House of Commons that extra-parliamentary campaigns, "agencies out of doors", were "the legitimate expressions of the people, by which bad legislation is to be corrected": cited by Patricia Hollis (ed.), *Pressure from Without in Early Victorian England* (1974), p. 5. Thirty, even twenty years earlier, this maxim would certainly not have been accepted either by him or by most politicians.

3. Elie Halévy, *A History of the English People in the Nineteenth Century,* III: *The Triumph of Reform, 1830–41* (Second edn., 1950), p. 65.

4. For O'Connell's family, his interests in land and his income from his practice at the Bar, see above all Maurice R. O'Connell, "Daniel O'Connell: income, expenditure and despair", *Irish Historical Studies*, XVII, No. 66 (Sept. 1970), 200–20. With his subsequent interests in newspapers and in the *Dublin Review*, in banking (he was a founder-director of the National Bank of Ireland) and in brewing as one of the chief investors in the O'Connell Brewery, an ultimately unsuccessful competitor of Guinness's Brewery, he was a thoroughly representative member of his class.

5. Vesey Fitzgerald to Peel, 5 July 1828, *Peel Memoirs*, I, 114–5, cited by Norman Gash, *Mr Secretary Peel* (1961), p. 522. Professor Gash, while principally concerned with Peel, provides also an authoritative account of the British political dimensions of the Catholic question which should be read in conjunction with G. I. T. Machin, *The Catholic Question in English Politics, 1820–30* (1964). For the history of the Catholic Association, James Reynolds, *The Catholic Emancipation Crisis in Ireland, 1823–29* (1954) is indispensable. The best general survey is R. B. McDowell, *Public Opinion and Government Policy in Ireland, 1801–46* (1952).

6. For his early life and intellectual formation, see Maurice R. O'Connell (ed.), *The Correspondence of Daniel O'Connell* (1972), I; and Arthur Houston (ed.), *Daniel O'Connell: His Early Life and Journal, 1795–1802* (1906). His period in London coincided with the government's attempts, at first only partly successful, to repress the English radical societies. In his letters home, O'Connell gave no hint of his increasingly liberal outlook—wisely, no doubt, in view of his expectations from his uncle Maurice O'Connell, "Old Hunting Cap", who was staunchly conservative.

7. Michael Brock, *The Great Reform Act* (1973), pp. 50–8, has provided an excellent account of the crisis over the Catholics. Emancipation, he concludes, "had an immense effect in advancing the cause of Reform".

8. Brock, pp. 58–60; J. Cannon, *Parliamentary Reform* (1973), p. 194.

9. Quoted by Cannon, p. 192.

10. For an account of the "Tithe War", involving fierce and sustained resistance throughout the country to the payment of this tax to the Established Church, see A. Macintyre, *The Liberator: Daniel O'Connell and the Irish Party, 1830–47* (1965), pp. 167–84.

11. Lord Mahon to Peel, 8 Jan. 1833, *Sir Robert Peel from his Private Papers,* ed. C. S. Parker (1891), II, 209–11.

12. Quoted by Brock, *The Great Reform Act*, p. 315.

13. D. O. Madden, *Ireland and its Rulers since 1829* (1843), I, 225–6; *Hansard*, Third Series, XV, cols. 148–77.
14. Robert Blake, *Disraeli* (1966), p. 131. For the feud between the two men, see *ibid*, pp. 124–6. The coarsely anti-Semitic tone of O'Connell's attack on Disraeli, as indefensible as Disraeli's own display of prejudice, was not characteristic: O'Connell supported Jewish emancipation.
15. On the Irish in Britain at this time, see T. W. Freeman, *Pre-Famine Ireland* (1957), pp. 37–50. According to the Census of 1841, there were 419,256 Irish-born people in Great Britain, but as Freeman remarks, this figure seriously underestimates the total Irish community. Children born in Britain of Irish-born parents "were not counted as Irish"; nor presumably does the figure adequately reflect the large numbers of seasonal migrants. More than one-tenth of the populations of Manchester, Liverpool and Glasgow and its neighbouring towns were Irish.
16. See Kevin B. Nowlan, *The Politics of Repeal* (1965), pp. 37–58.
17. O'Connell to FitzPatrick, 11 Feb. 1842, Maurice R. O'Connell (ed.), *The Correspondence of Daniel O'Connell* (1972–1980), VII, Letter 2941.
18. B. Disraeli, *Lord George Bentinck* (1852), pp. 159–60; *Hansard*, Third Series, LXXXIX, cols. 942–5.
19. W. E. Gladstone, in *The Nineteenth Century*, XXV, No. 43 (1889), pp. 149–68.

7

O'Connell's Impact on Europe

T. Desmond Williams

"I would like to have met three men only in this century: Napoleon, Cuvier and O'Connell." These few words—written by Balzac—testify in their fashion to the extraordinary impact left by O'Connell on European thought. There is no doubt that O'Connell attracted more attention on the continent of Europe than any other Irish leader in modern times.

To him civil liberty was every bit as important as religious. Like many other Irishmen he benefited indirectly from an age of revolution in which, as Tom Paine said, everything might be expected; but it was really the example of America, rather than France, that determined his early political outlook. Europe only comes in much later. He inherited much from the doctrines of the American Revolution—especially its egalitarian and libertarian attitudes. He by no means fully approved of the French Revolution though he was influenced by many of its ideas.

A number of points must be made clear at the outset. O'Connell's own vision rarely stretched with any intensity beyond the frontiers of Ireland and Westminster. Ireland lay always at the heart of his thoughts, though many Europeans—politicians, philosophers and journalists alike—envisaged him as a figure of universal interest. He was a very widely read man, well acquainted with French literature and law, and, within limits, with French history—certainly he knew a good deal more about it than most educated Irishmen or Englishmen of his age. This particular knowledge came largely from books. He did not travel widely in Europe, and such visits as he did make were extremely rare. America he never saw at all. Europeans came to him at Derrynane, or sought interviews in Dublin or London. He had received part of his education in France, though the type of education he received there was really designed for English Catholic gentlemen—at least such was the nature of the school and the attitude of the clergy who ran it. The only observable impact was the interest awoken, as mentioned, in various aspects of French culture. He also knew Latin; and his study of law must have given him a good command of theoretical principles concerning church and state relations and social justice. His language and actions often bore the stamp of tactical rather than strategic form. Mazzini put it that he had more emotion than "scienzia".

Odd little points arise. He was very much concerned, for instance, that none of his relatives should join the British army. If they were to join any army, it should be that of France or Austria. Yet he found this attitude quite compatible with loyalty to the Crown—within the framework of Repeal of the Union. His inclinations were monarchist—though he did on occasion use language that titillated advocates of republicanism in France and Italy. For example, he frequently offered a toast to the unity and liberty of Italy, so securing applause from Mazzini and his followers. For them and for radicals in other countries O'Connell represented, sometimes in its most elemental features, the cause in Ireland for which republicans were fighting elsewhere: namely that of the people against tyrants and kings. He certainly had no sympathy with Metternich, the Holy Alliance or the political system for which that great diplomat stood.

But then, in a sense, roles and attitudes were assigned to him which did not really concern him at all. His politics were essentially those of a moderate constitutional monarchist. French Liberal Catholics—Montalembert, Lacordaire and Lamennais—regarded him and his movement as models for political action in Europe. The movement also seemed to them a significant challenge to the power of England. Indeed, any continental states and parties opposed to English interests and influence tended to view O'Connell not only as a hero and champion of their causes but as a true rebel. For this very reason, Cavour, a great Anglophile, distrusted him. In the '30s and in the '40s—particularly between 1828 and 1845—his speeches in and outside Parliament received constant notice from the continental press. Ordinary German newspapers like the *Augsburger Allgemeine Zeitung* and the famous *Kolnische Zeitung* reported him almost weekly. It was not only the radical republicans who followed him; there were the Catholic groups too, engaged in conflict with the state. This was particularly true of the movements in the Rhineland in defence of predominantly Catholic interests against the Protestant state of Prussia, to which the Rhineland had been assigned at the Congress of Vienna. O'Connell was begged to intervene in Rome and at Westminster. The German Catholic Liberal leader, Goerres, was fascinated by his stand on relations between church and state, and his championing of the Liberal Catholic case in general. O'Connell's policy was naturally regarded as deeply critical of Metternich's intentions, in both domestic and external relations. He was also a hero to Czech and Slav nationalists who were struggling to gain a greater degree of self-government from the Hapsburgs and from Viennese bureaucracy.

In Europe, therefore, O'Connell was many things to many people. It was a period when liberalism and nationalism marched hand in hand, right up to 1848, the year of the futile revolutions, when so many long-standing alliances broke down. But at that stage O'Connell was gone: he never had to make the bitter choice between nationalism and liberty.

I have mentioned the Rhinelanders, the Slavs and the French. There were also the case of Poland and the Polish and Ruthenian revolutions of 1830 and 1846. Here O'Connell did intervene on several public occasions in quite a practical fashion. He supported the idea of a "free" and constitutionally governed Poland. But he was worried lest untimely support of the revolutionaries might encourage a futile rising and unnecessary bloodshed. Once at least he refrained from participating in an anti-Czarist demonstration in London. His sentiments about particular European causes were unquestionably sincere, but it is difficult to believe that any of them attracted him very deeply. His real passions centred around issues fought out in Ireland, and naturally, at Westminster. He never deliberately sought support from the continent, though so many there hoped for assistance from him.

O'Connell was obviously of considerable importance to the Holy See in its concern with Britain and the British Empire. The project of a British veto on the appointment of Catholic bishops in Ireland suited the Papacy. It also had wider implications concerning similar issues in Spain, France and Bielorussia. Liberal Catholics favoured a total separation of church and state. O'Connell had little sympathy with the vacillating manoeuvres of Gregory XVI though on one doctrinal issue—the revolutionary ideology of romantic nationalism—their views were not entirely dissimilar. Though he could well be held to have founded a nation on the union of Irish Catholic peasants and an Irish Catholic middle class, O'Connell was never a doctrinaire nationalist. Liberty was his prime concern, and Pope Gregory's denunciation of virtually all revolutionary activity that belonged to the new spirit of nationalism did not worry him unduly. It should perhaps be mentioned in passing that the establishment of an independent Belgium had their joint approval.

O'Connell also regarded the overthrow of Napoleon in 1815 as disastrous for the cause of liberty. But even so, at a period when Catholic Emancipation was being strongly resisted at Westminster, he never advocated disloyalty to the British Crown in its conflicts with foreign powers. And he detested much of 1789, particularly the persecution of the Church and the aggressive secularism of the Jacobins, though he fully approved of separation of church and state.

His name was quite well-known in Europe long before the Catholic Emancipation victory in 1829. The campaign for Emancipation had fired the imagination of Liberals in many countries, particularly in the newly Prussian Rhineland, France, Spain, Italy and Austria. He had fought and won a battle over the Veto, as it applied to Ireland, but the practice of state intervention in ecclesiastical appointments was common to most states, Protestant as well as Catholic. O'Connell's victory on this issue naturally aroused irritation in European conservative circles, as it did far more obviously in England. But the period of his greatest impact was the late '30s and the early '40s, the latter being the years of the Repeal movement.

European Catholics in general had admired and supported the campaign for Emancipation. But reaction to attempts to repeal the Act of Union was far more mixed. The issue had many political overtones. Catholics were divided into liberals and conservatives. Most conservatives looked to Britain for support in their conflict against the forces of revolution in Europe—though indeed they did not always receive her support. By these O'Connell was regarded as a revolutionary figure, however much they may have admired his emancipatory zeal. There were some who greatly feared his effect on the *status quo* in their own countries, still governed on the principles of the *Ancien Regime*. Among these conservative critics was a very influential German publicist, Karl von Jahrcke: he was deeply sceptical of the consequences of O'Connell's mass meetings, and the association of the Repeal movement with what could well prove to be an outright attack on the principle of private property and indeed of state stability. Jahrcke was a very civilised man; and despite his conservatism, he contributed quite frequently to the liberal journal edited by Goerres—Historisch Politische Blatter, the policy of which was generally pro-O'Connell. It was however the great Metternich who feared O'Connell's influence above all others. He constantly expressed his alarm to the Vatican and to Britain, stressing the dangers to conservative society and to the Church's international interests. Innumerable dispatches on the subject travelled between the Papacy and Vienna, and London and Vienna, throughout 1843 and 1844. Metternich appears even more of an alarmist than Gregory XVI or the latter's two leading diplomatic advisers, Cardinals Lambruschini and Fransoni. The great master of conservative diplomacy was especially indignant over what he denounced as the intervention of the Church in Ireland on the side of popular agitation, which he naturally equated with revolutionary ideas (there were, as it happened, several Irish bishops who felt the same way).

Throughout the whole period revolution was a constant threat to the Vatican and to the Hapsburgs. The success of any such activity in Ireland would only, in their view, spark off something similar, though far more disastrous, at their own palace gates. Gregory XVI was particularly concerned, as mentioned earlier, with revolutionary movements in Poland, Belgium, and in his own Papal States. He tried very hard to keep the clergy out of public affairs in politically sensitive areas, wherever they might be tempted to identify with national, liberal or social aspirations. Even though Papal concern was expressed over the social and ecclesiastical grievances, which O'Connell was so anxious to alleviate, the Irish clergy were frequently warned—with a steady flow of promptings from London, Florence, St Petersburg and Rome—against encouraging their flocks in any way to support O'Connell. This was a very difficult directive, and it received from the Irish bishops far from whole-hearted obedience: the Archbishop of Tuam, MacHale, made no effort to conceal his defiance. In the European conservative view, backed by a somewhat disconcerted Papacy, O'Connell was regarded as both hero and anti-hero. So, whether he liked it or not, or even whether he knew it or not, he was involved in the intricate diplomacy of many foreign powers.

England loomed large in the formation of Papal policy. There were a good many Catholics who looked to England as a bulwark against the expansion of heretical powers such as Czarist Russia. They also viewed England as fundamentally opposed to the forces of extreme liberalism and socialism. They therefore favoured the preservation of the union between Great Britain and Ireland, and were indeed disturbed by any hint of waning English authority in any part of the world. They also wanted England re-Catholicised. On this issue there was no need to worry about Ireland, but they did not wish to see any confrontation between England and the Holy See. In fact these Catholics regarded English support, along with that of Metternich, as essential for the maintenance of the temporal power of the Papacy.

There were times when O'Connell's remarks could not but be interpreted in the continent as clearly in favour of radical movements. I have mentioned earlier the benevolent if slightly patronising support provided by Mazzini. As to Spain, the ferocity of O'Connell's attacks on Don Carlos and the Traditionalists created great dismay in conservative and clerical quarters, even causing Rome to question his religions orthodoxy. On the other hand, his ultimate objectives in Ireland were considered acceptable if not necessarily to be admired. There was general approval in particular of his efforts to secure Emancipation, and to follow it up in the relevant social and political arenas. The heart of the problem lay in the fact that the Papacy disapproved of his intermediary tactics. He had become a highly resourceful architect of democratic and liberal ambitions. There were conservatives who side-stepped this unfortunate development by making a sharp distinction between "agitation" in Ireland and its equivalent on the continent. O'Connell's masterly deployment of all the available forces of mass propaganda was accepted by them as the inevitable outcome of the Irish historical past for which the English government and the Irish Protestant Church had to bear responsibility.

To most liberals he remained the great hero of popular Catholic if not republican ideology. Nearly all the German Catholic writers, with the exception of Jahrcke, supported his enterprises without reservation. So, of course, did the French, and above all, Montalembert. And Lamennais and his followers continued to sing his praises, even after they had broken with the Papacy.

To return for a moment to Metternich: he was also worried about the whole concept of popular movements, having in mind the nationalistic "contradictions" stirring already within the Hapsburg dominions. Dissident Slav elements were thrusting their way to the surface in the 1840s. Havlicek and Palacky, the founders of modern Czech nationalism, saw to it that glowing reports of O'Connell's progress appeared in the local Prague newspapers. They also regarded the repeal of the Union and the establishment of two kingdoms in Ireland, under a common monarch, as providing a possible model for the solution of the Bohemian question.

The theme of the obituary sermon in Rome by Ventura, the leader of the Liberal Catholics in Italy, was the relationship between the Church and freedom. He lauded O'Connell as the foremost exponent of the union between religion and liberty; as the first statesman to understand and implement the principles of civil independence and true freedom. Now a close adviser to the young and as yet liberal Pius IX, Ventura went so far as to say that if governments refused to concede freedom to the Church and religious liberty to their peoples, the Church would turn her back on them in favour of democracy which she would then baptise. This was going a good deal further than Pius or possibly even O'Connell would have gone. While on this subject it is appropriate to observe that Cavour, though he disliked O'Connell, paid him the compliment of taking over his fundamental idea of a free church in a free state.

In conclusion one may point to four comments on O'Connell, each of some special interest. On his death Pius IX described him as "the great champion of the Church, the father of his people and the glory of the whole Christian world". A German coachman told a tourist that he was "the man who discovered Ireland". Bismarck said: "O'Connell was a man I think I would have had shot." And Macaulay wrote:

> Go where you will on the Continent, visit any cofee-house, dine at any table, embark upon any steamboat, enter any conveyance—from the moment your accent shows you to be an Englishman, the very first question you are asked by your companions, be they advocates, merchants, manufacturers, physicians or peasants like our yeomen, is: "What is to be done with O'Connell?"

8

O'Connell: Lawyer and Landlord

Maurice R. O'Connell

In folklore Daniel O'Connell is known as the Counsellor. He was given this title by tradition because of his success as an advocate in defending humble people against laws and court prosecutions which they saw as unjust. He was only known as the Liberator late in life, a title bestowed by his political followers. It was his skill as a lawyer which made him widely known, and prepared the ground for his rise to political leadership.

Having pursued his legal studies in London and Dublin he was called to the Irish Bar in April 1798. Like most barristers he had little business at first but by 1805 he was achieving distinction. By 1813 he was making nearly £4,000 a year which meant that he was in the front rank of his profession. In the 1820s his earnings reached a peak of £7,000 and averaged nearly £6,000 a year.

As a Catholic O'Connell was prevented by the Penal Laws from being promoted to the Inner Bar, that is, becoming a King's Counsel (K.C. for short). He estimated that he would have earned an additional thousand pounds a year had the law allowed him this honour; and being a K.C. would have saved him from a certain amount of drudgery. He felt keenly having to remain a junior barrister.

Living in Dublin and practising at the Four Courts he was a member of the Munster Bar. This involved attending the assizes at Ennis, Limerick, Tralee and Cork for five or six weeks twice a year, in the spring and the late summer. When he was away on circuit he and his wife wrote to each other four or five times a week, and most of what we know of his day-to-day legal practice comes from these letters.

He enjoyed his profession, once telling his wife from the Cork assizes that "you know how I love the bustle of the courts".[1] Years later she told him:

> I ought not, darling, regret so much your going circuit for in general the change and bustle of it is of use to you. It completely does away any little *hippishness* [depression] you may have.

He liked to tell his wife of his courtroom triumphs and of the volume of legal business he was doing. In 1811 he wrote from Cork:

> My success this circuit has been great, very great. I have that vanity which makes me think I have made an *impression*. You will not laugh at me though anybody else would.

On another occasion he wrote from Ennis:

> There is an immense deal of business here and I do believe not only that I have as much as any barrister but more, *a great deal more*. Indeed this is as usual a famous town for business. There is a most laudable spirit of litigation.

Again, he told his wife:

> All my prisoners have been acquitted. The dock alone has produced me a small fortune. I had the County Court-house this day for near an hour in a roar of laughter at a witness whom I examined, the judge, jury and all the spectators. I have always remarked that nothing advances an Irish barrister more than the talent of ridicule.

A murder case in which he was the defence counsel has found its way into literature. The murder became the theme of Gerald Griffin's novel, *The Collegians*, and later of Dion Boucicault's play, *The Colleen Bawn*, eventually becoming the subject of Julius Benedict's opera, *The Lily of Killarney*. O'Connell's version was more prosaic:

> You will be surprised to hear that I had a client convicted yesterday for a murder for whom I fought a hard battle, and yet I do not feel any the most slight regret at his conviction. It is very unusual with me to be *so* satisfied, but he is a horrid villain. In the first place he got a creature, a lovely creature of fifteen, to elope with him from her uncle who brought her up an orphan and to rob him of his all, 100 guineas, and in three weeks after he contrived to get her into a boat on the Shannon with his servant, said when he returned to Glin that he left her at Kilrush, then reported she had gone off with a sea captain, and she was not heard of afterwards for near two months when a mutilated carcase floated on shore or rather was thrown, which was identified to be hers from some extremely re-markable teeth. He will be hanged tomorrow unless being a gentle-man prevents him.

The murderer was hanged the following day.

careful to evade indictment. He then launched another insulting attack on the Attorney-General's conduct and character.

In his brilliant study, *The King of the Beggars*, Seán O'Faoláin pays special attention to O'Connell's handling of the Magee trial, and then he adds:

> Everybody, indeed, who regards gracious living, nobility in thought and word and behaviour, must read this demagogue with a curl of distaste... Heaven knows, they may well do so, for O'Connell did a great deal to kill gentle manners in Ireland, to vulgarise and cheapen us.[4]

But, O'Faoláin maintains, O'Connell had no alternative if he were to raise a people from their knees.

Peel was not the only man who thought O'Connell had gone too far. That view was also held by O'Connell's uncle at Derrynane, Muirish an Chaipín or Maurice of the Cap, known to posterity as Hunting-Cap. He wrote his nephew a reprimand:

> However averse and hostile the Attorney-General may be to the Catholics... the high situation he enjoys as first law officer of the Crown demands a degree of respect and consideration from the bar which should not be lightly forgot or neglected.

After more in the same strain Hunting-Cap delivered his instructions for the future:

> I have therefore most earnestly to request, and will even add, to insist, that you will in future conduct yourself with calmness, temperance and moderation towards him, and that you will not suffer yourself to be hurried by hate or violence of passions to use any language unbecoming the calm and intelligent barrister or the judicious and well-bred gentleman.

Hunting-Cap then expressed his disapproval of the way O'Connell had played to the gallery:

> The flattering power of popular applause has often subdued reason and laid people to acts for which they severely suffered but believe me, my dear friend, it has ever proved a very perishable commodity. No man of solid sense will ever be anxious to look for or obtain it.

This was the aristocratic eighteenth century expressing its disdain, not so much for the bourgeois nineteenth as for the democracy of the twentieth.

Had O'Connell followed his uncle's orders and behaved like a gentleman he would probably have gone down in history as that very able barrister who assisted Lord Fingall, the leader of the Catholic aristocracy, in an unsuccessful struggle for Emancipation. Instead, the demagogue drove the Catholic aristocracy—the men of gentle manners—out of politics, and by organising the people he served notice on the Catholic gentry that political leadership must be earned. The Forty-Shilling Freeholders were not the only Catholics to find the chalice of Emancipation laced with vinegar. But Fingall was not soured. On his deathbed in 1836 he asked to have O'Connell informed that the Catholic aristocracy, including himself, had been "criminally cowardly", and he continued:

> We never understood that we had a nation behind us—O'Connell alone comprehended that properly, and he used his knowledge fitly. It was by him the gates of the Constitution were broken open for us; we owe everything to his rough work, and, to effect further services for Ireland, there must be more of it.[5]

It is surprising to learn that in the early stages of his career nearly all his clients in civil cases—the profitable side of the legal profession—were Protestants. Catholics feared to employ a co-religionist, particularly one so aggressively political. He furnished this information in evidence before a select committee of the House of Lords in 1825:

> The Roman Catholics had a kind of feeling that they were not quite so secure in the courts (I mean this not to apply to judges, but to the entire machinery) as the Protestants. They, the Catholics, did not like to increase the disfavour by having a Catholic advocate; and there are reasons connected with myself of perhaps more animation, I would call it, and others intemperance, which made them particularly desirous to avoid me; so that I got into professional business by my clients being generally and almost exclusively Protestants.

The question immediately arises that if Catholics were afraid to engage him in civil suits, how did he build up his reputation in folklore as the great defence counsel of humble Catholics in criminal cases (his letters to his wife show that he did most of the criminal business on the Munster circuit)? Why were Catholics not afraid to employ him in criminal cases? The answer to this question is indicated in one of the speeches he made in the House of Commons on the Coercion Bill of 1834:

I have, in the course of my life, defended as Counsel a greater number of the perpetrators of these [agrarian] outrages, than of any other class of offenders; but I never asked a question in cross-examination, an answer to which could bring out a fact or an opinion tending to mitigate the crime. My defence always supposed the prisoner innocent of the charge, but I never attempted to mitigate the atrocity of the crime. I never quitted an assize town at which Whiteboys were tried, without addressing the public publicly, and expressing my abhorrence of the crime as well as explaining the injurious effects which it occasioned to those who were engaged in its commission.[6]

This declaration can be accepted as true since he had a hatred of violence, agrarian and political, and he expressed that hatred in private as well as public at every stage of his career. Since he felt so deeply on the subject he must have been able to convince the courts of his sincerity in condemning the crime while absolving his client. Thus judges and other court personnel and juries could see him impartially as a criminal lawyer.

And finally, one must consider what sort of a barrister O'Connell really was, not just how he behaved in great dramas like the Magee trial but how he behaved on normal occasions, and what kind of a legal mind did he have. The historian finds it difficult to answer these questions directly because it is impossible to judge a barrister from newspaper accounts of trials: he must look to contemporary or near-contemporary witnesses. The present writer has found two whose evidence is impressive, one a contemporary barrister, William Henry Curran,[7] a son of the celebrated John Philpot Curran, the other a young observer of the political scene in O'Connell's last years, Daniel Owen Madden.[8] A third witness to whom one turns is J. Roderick O'Flanagan who was called to the Irish Bar in 1838. Unfortunately, his *The Bar Life of O'Connell* is too anecdotal, and for his more analytical comments he leans on Madden.

Curran sees O'Connell's knowledge of the law in all kinds of court cases as comprehensive but practical rather than scholarly. He and Madden agree that O'Connell was unrivalled as an advocate in all kinds of law but especially in jury cases. They admire his physical and mental energy, his pertinacity and resource; and while allowing for his ingenuity and apparent play-acting they see him as always cautious. They also agree that he had an acute understanding of the Irish mind which he used to brilliant effect in cross-examining witnesses and appealing to juries, and even in playing on a judge's weaknesses.

Two quotations from their publications are worthy of mention. One expresses Curran's opinion of O'Connell's handling of juries:

> Throw him upon any particular class of men, and you would imagine that he must have lived among them all his life, so intuitively does he accommodate his style of arguments to their particular modes of thinking and reasoning.

Madden was too young to have seen O'Connell perform in court but he must have known barristers old enough to have done so, and he did have some legal training. Though he despised O'Connell as a political leader he admired his skill as a lawyer. In describing O'Connell's conduct when he had a weak case, he says:

> He acted the part of an indignant lawyer to perfection; caught up his brief-bag in a seeming fury, and dashed it against the witness table—frowned—muttered fearfully to himself—sat down in a rage, with a horrid scowl on his face; bounced up again, in a fit of boiling passion, and solemnly protested in the face of heaven against such injustice—threw his brief away—swaggered out of the Court House—then swaggered back again, and wound up by browbeating and abusing half-a-dozen more witnesses, and without any real grounds whatever, finally succeeded in making half the jury refuse to bring in a verdict of "Guilty".

The passages contains obvious exaggeration but must not be seen as caricature. When one remembers O'Connell's outrageous conduct in the Magee trial one can see him behaving in a manner approaching Madden's colourful description.

After the end of the Cork assizes in September each year O'Connell used to take a month's holiday in Kerry. He would visit relatives and friends there, particularly in the peninsula that runs out into the Atlantic from Killarney. That peninsula is mountainous and weather-beaten tourist country, the Barony of Iveragh comprising its remote western part. O'Connell's rich uncle, Hunting-Cap, lived at Derrynane on the south–west corner of the peninsula while O'Connell's parents lived some twenty miles north, close to the hamlet that he helped develop into the small town of Cahirciveen. The O'Connells were the principal family in Iveragh for some centuries before O'Connell was born in 1775. His family property and his dreams were centred in that part of the world.

On the death of his father in 1809 he fell in for an estate with a rental of about £2,000 though this figure fell to less than £1,500 when peace came after the end of the Napoleonic Wars. On Hunting-Cap's death in 1825 his estate was divided more or less equally between O'Connell and his two brothers. Thus from 1825 onwards O'Connell had an income from land of about £4,000 a year.

Extravagant and open-handed he was always in debt. Generous to poor relations, he was a "soft touch", lending money too freely and going security for people who sometimes let him down. His wife feared his journeys to Iveragh because of the money he would dispense there. He contributed much to charitable institutions.[9]

Kerry tradition has it that he was a good landlord, easy on his tenants when times were bad, and never known to evict. His letters and other evidence support this tradition but they also show that it is inaccurate: it needs to be qualified.

In 1812 he told his wife:

> The rents are coming in extremely fast without the smallest trouble as the poor people have a most abundant year of it. Indeed at all times my rents are comfortably paid as I would not consent to have any creature put himself under more rent than the land was well worth.

Rents were easy to pay during the Napoleonic Wars, when agricultural produce fetched high prices, but a depression set in afterwards which lasted many years. Matters got worse when a famine hit the country in 1822. O'Connell expressed his concern in a letter to his daughter Kate:

> There is nothing but grief and woe in Kerry. The people starving and the gentry in bitter want. No rents, no money, the fever and famine raging. May the great God be merciful to them all.

Six months later he instructed his land agent to send him up any rents he could collect but he cautioned him against being severe. By 1825 normal times had returned, and he took a stronger line on collecting his rents, threatening to evict if necessary. Three weeks later, however, he adopted a more lenient tone.

In 1834 Kerry was struck by cholera, and in letters to his agent O'Connell showed the deepest concern. He instructed him to spare no expense: engage a physician to go around the villages and houses; supply poor families with medicines, bread and meat, and with coal and blankets for warmth; and see that special Masses and other public prayers were said to "avert the Divine Wrath". His correspondence shows the same solicitude during the Great Famine. In almost daily communication with the Government's Famine Relief Office in Dublin he arranged for the transport of food to Cahirciveen; and he purchased food at his own expense for distribution to his tenants.

In the middle of the Tithe War in 1832 he ordered his agent to evict a certain tenant and that tenant's near relatives if it were true that he had driven cattle for the local Protestant curate, Rev. Francis Chute. The cattle, O'Connell believed, had been distrained by Chute for non-payment of tithes. His action was autocratic since the man's conduct had nothing to do with his tenancy. The proposed eviction, however, would have won popular approval since any man assisting the tithe-collector was regarded as a public enemy. The Iveragh poet, Tomás Ruadh Ó Súilleabháin, wrote a poem about this time which deals with a widow whose cow was distrained for non-payment of tithes by this very curate.[10] The feeling expressed in the poem shows that Ó Súilleabháin would have applauded the eviction of any cattle-driver employed in the collection of tithes.

In his evidence before the Devon Commission in 1845 O'Connell said:

> I make it an invariable rule never to dispossess a tenant, unless he has misconducted himself in some way, such as by running in debt and ruining himself totally with other persons, dissipating his property in that way; or some flagrant crime, so that a man would not wish to have such a person on his property. For the last thirty-eight years I have not dispossessed any one for any other reasons, and very few at all.[11]

The evidence shown in the above-mentioned letters to his agent, and his statement to the Devon Commission, show that O'Connell was prepared to evict, and on occasion, did evict. Yet Kerry tradition has it that he was never known to evict. Can this contradiction be resolved? Probably it can. In Irish tradition the word eviction has a perjorative implication. It usually means the unjust ejectment of a tenant. Ejectment for failure to pay a reasonable rent, when that failure was the tenant's own fault, would not be regarded as an eviction in this special sense. As long as ejectments ordered by O'Connell did not offend local opinion he would not be thought of as an evicting landlord. However, his instructions to his agent concerning the tenant believed guilty of driving distrained cattle, and his evidence before the Devon Commission, prove that his interpretation of the rights and duties of a landlord were more paternalistic than one would expect in a democratic leader.

O'Connell's land agent from 1822 to 1845 was his cousin, John Primrose, Jr., a native of Iveragh. According to local tradition he was a proud man and unpopular with the tenants.[12] In his biography of O'Connell in Irish, Domnaill Ó Súilleabháin, who was well versed in Iveragh tradition, says that the tenants were afraid to complain to O'Connell of his agent's oppressions through fear of incurring the agent's displeasure. Ó Súilleabháin adds, however, that the tenants did not blame O'Connell for his agent's actions.[13] Since O'Connell mixed freely with the people every autumn at patterns (the annual celebration of a parish's patron saint), races and beagling, it is impossible to believe that his tenants would not have made their grievances known to him. That they did make such reports is shown by a letter in which he reproved Primrose on an estate matter and then added that "all the other tenants would be sure to complain to me privately of your giving preferences according to your interest and would so complain even without any substantial cause". In spite of Ó Súilleabháin's statement to the contrary, O'Connell must have known what his tenants thought of Primrose but he may well have seen in an unpopular agent a useful antidote to his own "softness" and open-handedness. For all his warmth and spontaneity he could be very calculating.

O'Connell's reputation as a landlord came under fire in a series of letters in *The Times* in 1845. It had commissioned one of its journalists, Thomas Campbell Foster, to tour Ireland and write an account of conditions there. He spent three months on his travels, and published his findings in weekly letters in *The Times* as he went along. In these he made adverse criticisms of many landlords, naming O'Connell as probably the worst.[14] He contended that O'Connell charged unjustly high rents, that a great many of his tenants lived in squalor, that he did nothing to improve the farming on his estate, and that he allowed excessive subdivision in order to win an easy popularity. He did not accuse him, however, of being an evicting landlord which was the charge above all others likely to destroy a landlord's reputation in Ireland.

O'Connell reacted with characteristic energy and vituperation, denouncing Foster as the "gutter commissioner of the Times" and as a "boundless liar".[15] Stung by these and other epithets, Foster surpassed O'Connell in scurrility, labelling him a political "imposter" and "mountbank", and the son of a huckster shopkeeper whose family were of disreputable origin. Needless to say, O'Connell denied or ridiculed most of the charges, and mentioned among other things in his favour that he had allowed many tenants evicted from other estates to settle on his.

As a check on Foster's findings a second representative of *The Times* visited Kerry. He was William Howard Russell who later achieved fame as a war correspondent in the Crimea. He corroborated Foster's account, both men paying particular attention to the squalor in which the tenants lived in the townland of Derrynane Beg, close to O'Connell's home in the townland of Derrynane Mor. Russell reported that Derrynane Beg comprised sixty-two holdings, the rents varying from £7 a year for the largest to two shillings a year for the smallest.[16] When one realises that there are only six holdings in the townland today, none of them economically viable, one can understand what conditions must have been like in 1845. In his memoirs written about 1890 Russell returned to the subject:

> I believe the tenants of Derrynanebeg were squatters, the evicted refuse of adjoining estates, who flocked to the boggy valley, where they were allowed to run up their hovels of soddened earth and mud, with leave to turn out their lean kine and cultivate patches of potatoes on the hillside, paying as many shillings as the agent could squeeze out of them.[17]

Foster's point that O'Connell allowed his tenants to subdivide their holdings at will in order to achieve an easy popularity ignored that fact that it was very difficult for a landlord to prevent subdivision unless he pursued a policy of eviction as a result of which his tenants would regard him as a tyrant. The accusation of neglect overlooked the fact that a very busy public life and an incurable tendency to live beyond his means meant that O'Connell had neither the time nor the capital for substantial investment in his property.

Foster paid particular attention to Cahirciveen, the hamlet which O'Connell developed into a small town of about one thousand people. Foster wrote of "the wretched looking town of Cahirciveen, its dirty unpaved streets, and old-hat-mended windows". O'Connell retorted that he had spent £4,000 on donations and improvements to the town, and had given perpetual leases for sites for the building of houses at almost nominal rents. Since he itemised most of these benefactions it can be taken that he spoke the substantial truth. Had he lied, everybody in his beloved Iveragh would have known that he lied. Furthermore, Cahirciveen tradition has it that he was a generous landlord to the town.[18]

He did have an English defender—the young Quaker, W. E. Forster (to be Chief Secretary for Ireland at the time of Parnell). He came to Ireland in September 1846 to investigate famine conditions for the English quakers who were about to send a relief expedition. He spent two nights with O'Connell at Derrynane, and wrote home from north Kerry a few days later:

I have made a great deal of inquiry in all quarters respecting his tenantry, and I am convinced that the impression made by the report in *The Times* is most unfair and untrue. I should say he is decidedly the best landlord in his district. but owing to his having allowed ejected tenants from other properties to squat on his estate at nominal rents, there are, of course some wretched cabins.[19]

One can say in conclusion that O'Connell was a very popular landlord, but since he employed a land agent disliked by the tenants, that popularity was largely but not fully deserved. Though generous to Cahirciveen, in the development of which he took pride, he neglected his estate as a whole except in times of hardship. For that neglect there were extenuating circumstances in his busy public life and his extravagance. It must be owned, however, that a great many Irish landlords were short of investment capital so that his neglect would not have elicited from Irishmen the harsh judgments passed by English visitors. Taking all factors into account one can say that O'Connell was a reasonably good landlord.

Notes

1. All letters quoted or referred to in this article are published in Maurice R. O'Connell, (ed.), *The Correspondence of Daniel O'Connell*, (Dublin, 1972–1980). Since they can easily be identified in the published volumes they are not footnoted in this article.

2. Peel to Viscount Whitworth (successor as Lord-Lieutenant to Richmond), 1 August 1813, Charles S. Parker, (ed.), *Sir Robert Peel*, (London, 1891), I, p. 104.

3. Peel to the Earl of Desart, 10 August 1813, Parker, *Peel*, I, pp. 116–117.

4. Seán O'Faoláin, *The King of the Beggars*, (London, 1938), p. 204.

5. William Fagan, *The Life and Times of Daniel O'Connell*, (Cork, 1847), I, p. 162.

6. *Mirror of Parliament*, 1834, pp. 2849–2850. This report has O'Connell using the word "Whitefeet" instead of "Whiteboys" but he must have used, and he certainly meant to use, the latter term. The description "Whitefeet" was not used before 1830, by which time O'Connell had retired from the Bar. Furthermore, *Hansard* (3rd Series, XXV, p. 296), in a shorter version of his speech, uses the term "Whiteboyism", not "Whitefeet", in its report. O'Connell made a speech of this kind after the conclusion of the Doneraile Conspiracy trials.

7. William Henry Curran, "Sketches of the Irish Bar—Mr. O'Connell", *New Monthly Magazine*, Vol. 8 (1823).

8. Daniel Owen Madden, *Ireland and its Rulers since 1829*, (London, 1844), I, pp. 22–5.

9. This account of O'Connell's financial position comes from my article, "Daniel O'Connell: income, expenditure and despair", *Irish Historical Studies*, (Sept. 1970), XVII, No. 66, 200–220.

10. "An gheadach d'a crudhadh 'san Ghleann", in Séamus Fenton, *Amhráin Thómais Ruaidh, i., The Songs of Tomás Ruadh O'Sullivan, the Iveragh Poet, 1785–1848*, (Dublin, 1914, second edition, 1922), No. XXVII. I am indebted to Dr. Pádraig de Brún for bringing this poem to my attention.

11. *Evidence taken before Her Majesty's Commissioners of Enquiry into the State of the Law and Practice in respect to the Occupation of Land in Ireland*, (Dublin, 1845), Part III, p. 936. O'Connell gave his evidence on 28 January 1845.

12. I am indebted to the late Eugene Ring of Main St., Cahirciveen for the local tradition on Primrose as a land agent.

13. *Beatha Domnaill Ui Chonaill*, (Baile Atha Cliath, 1936), p. 198.

14. Foster's strictures on O'Connell appeared in *The Times* of November 18, December 3 and 25, and January 6.

15. O'Connell defended himself in speeches in the Repeal Association on November 24, December 1, 8, 15 and 29, and January 5.

16. Russell's report appeared in *The Times* of 25 December 1845.

17. John B. Atkins, *The Life of Sir William Howard Russell*, (London, 1911), I, pp. 33–34.

18. I am indebted to Sister M. de Lourdes of the Presentation Convent in Cahirciveen, for much information on O'Connell's relations with Cahirciveen.

19. T. Wemyss Reid, Life of the Rt. Hon. W. E. Forster, (London, 1888), I, pp. 178–81.